The Bickersons
A Biography Of Radio's Wittiest Program

The Bickersons
A Biography Of Radio's Wittiest Program

By Ben Ohmart

Foreword by
Frances Langford

BearManor Media
2013

The Bickersons: A Biography of Radio's Wittiest Program
© 2004 by Ben Ohmart. All rights reserved.
2nd printing, 2013

Foreword © 2004 by Frances Langford
Star Time, *The Old Gold Show*, and *The Bickersons* scripts © 2004 by Paul Rapp
"The Rapp Writing Team Closes Generation Gap" © 1967 by Joel Rapp

"You Say It (But You Won't Do It)" Words and music by Alan Spilton and Gloria Shayne
© 1962 by Daywin Music, Inc. Copyright renewed.
All Rights Administered by Careers-BMG Music Publishing, Inc.
International Copyright Secured. All Rights Reserved

Published in the USA by

BearManor Media
P. O. Box 71426
Albany, GA 31708

bearmanormedia.com

Cover design & cartoon illustrations by Lloyd W. Meek
Typesetting and layout by John Teehan

Library of Congress Cataloging-in-Publication Data

Ohmart, Ben.
The Bickersons : a biography of radio's wittiest program /
by Ben Ohmart ; foreword by Frances Langford.
p. cm.
Includes bibliographical references and index.
ISBN 1-59393-008-9 (alk. paper)

1. Bickersons (Radio program) I. Title.

PN1991.77.B43O45 2005
791.44'72--dc22
2004029735

ISBN—1-59393-008-9
978-1-59393-008-0

For Paul Rapp

The reason for this book

Table of Contents

Foreword by Frances Langford i

Introduction..1

John and Blanche Bickerson 5

The Honeymoon Is Over: A History of The Bickersons 23

It's *Star Time!* 69

The 1951 Series...111

The Honeymoon(ers) Is Over 115

Bickering and Pitching 125

Recording Stars 133

Match Please, Darling 147

And More Commercials 167

Very Animated 173

The Final Years and Beyond 177

Philip Rapp 195

Don Ameche 199

Frances Langford 203

Lew Parker 209

Marsha Hunt...215

Virginia Grey 219

Danny Thomas 223

Unused Material...225

Index...253

Foreword
by Frances Langford

My initial thought when I first read my first Bickersons script was: I don't think I can do this. Because I wasn't used to that sort of thing. I had done a lot of little bits with Bob Hope on our tours entertaining the troops, which was very easy and fun. I learned a lot from Bob, about timing and comedy.

But I was scared to death during the first broadcast of the Bickersons, and at the same time I loved doing it. Not knowing where the laughs come and not knowing how funny it was going to be—it was all shocking. I practically memorized all the scripts, and it took me a while to get used to John and Blanche, but how I did love it.

Much of this was due to the incredible professionalism and brilliance of Don Ameche and Phil Rapp.

Don Ameche was something else. He was the greatest actor, and knew his lines backwards. The minute he walked onto the set, he knew his lines, my lines and everything. It was so wonderful working with him. He could do anything. If you can snore like that, you can do *anything*!

Phil Rapp, our writer/producer/director, was amazing. To me, he was the perfect director for what we were doing. The scripts were lively and clever. They were the best scripts I had ever read. It was a delight to bring them to life.

It's been a lot of years since I've done the Bickersons, but I still get fan mail from it, and lots of people

Don, Phil and Frances.

are still laughing at it, even the kids. I think it's timeless humor. Though we really played it for laughs more than any social significance, I think families are just the same now as they were in the 1940s. Maybe everyone isn't married to a Bickerson, but every upcoming generation that listens to the Bickersons seems to get quite a chuckle out of that shrew Blanche, and poor husband John.

It's a sheer delight to have been a part of a major comedy team like the Bickersons. I'm so sorry Don had to go; I'd like to do the Bickersons today. But as long as the shows keep circulating, and new fans continue to write me and share the laughs, it's a foregone conclusion that The Honeymoon Will Never Be Over...

– Frances Langford
January 2004

Introduction

I was probably 8 or 9 when I first heard The Bickersons. It was just one tape of several in a set of comedy recordings you could find at any bookstore in the country. I've no idea why I or my mother bought it, but that incredible cassette is my first memory of a lifelong love of old-time radio. The writing was flawless, the performances were like nothing I'd experienced before. Frances Langford played the insufferable Blanche Bickerson while poor husband John, victim of Contagious Insomnia, or Schmoo's Disease, was portrayed by Don Ameche. The battling couple would frequently go at it at 2 in the morning when John's incredible, whining, giggling, tumultuous snoring would cause Blanche to wake him up. They would fight about everything from relatives to Nature Boy (the cat) to sexy siren Gloria Gooseby to 90-pound babies.

John worked his life away selling bowling balls or running a streetcar or any menial job he could get. It was exhausting. All he wanted to do was come home and get some sleep before the whole rotten cycle started itself again. At least he had one good friend to help him through troubled times. Bourbon—via his Bottle of the Month Club from Kentucky.

Meanwhile, Blanche would employ herself by robbing the sugar bowl of the rent money to buy bald minks and new hats, causing no end of strife when the bills came due. The compulsive-impulsive type, Mrs. Bickerson didn't think often about the future, except how she would look in a new dress. But more than anything, she just wanted sleepy John's attention.

In the early days, one of the recurring troubles was the scheming mind of Blanche's brother Amos (played by Danny Thomas) who would come up with some crazy graft that would set Amos free from work but which would cost John his sanity. Blanche would typically give John's clothes to Amos if he had a United Nations Pool Hall appointment. Luckily, John was always so tired he could end his misery, at least for a time, by just shutting those heavy eyelids of his.

Still, somehow, the Bickersons kept together for at least 8 years, and probably a lot longer. It was a real love-hate relationship that, in moments of extreme hardship, showed that John and Blanche really loved one another, despite the snoring, the lack of money and the craziness of all those grasping friends and relatives around them.

Audiences of the 1950s were lucky to view a wealth of TV appearances by the Bickersons. They appeared on *The Ed Sullivan Show*; six times on *The Steve Allen Show*; five times on *The Perry Como Show* from 1958 to 1960; twice on *Hollywood Palace* in 1959; once on *The Jack Carson Show* in 1958; and six times on Sid Caesar's shows from 1955 to 1959. When Don Ameche was unavailable to play John, Lew Parker would step in, and the reviews were always the same: raves.

Even after more than 50 years on radio, records and CDs, the Bickersons are just as popular now as they were then, exciting new generations to laugh at John and Blanche and the woes of marriage. And to laugh at themselves. Timeless comedy, without a doubt.

Luck and Langford are the reasons you're reading this today. If it were not for the graciousness of Frances Langford responding to my letter in 2001, there would not be two volumes of Bickersons scripts or this book on the market. She put me in touch with Phil Rapp's son Paul who lavished a generosity on me that I think few strangers have ever experienced in their lives. Though I live a whole country away (CA to PA), Paul sent me his father's *entire* output of scripts, letters and papers, *at his expense*, for me to wade through at my leisure. To a true fan, this is the ultimate heaven and compliment, and it is why the book is dedicated to him. Thanks for the trust and selflessness, Paul.

There was so much material (mostly scripts, especially Baby Snooks) to go through, the entire story of everyone involved obviously could not be covered in this one minute volume. Therefore, during the course of my research, I branched out into a few other biographies. For the *whole* story on Don Ameche, you may want to read *Don Ameche, The Kenosha Comeback Kid*. And Philip Rapp's life and work were just too prolific to compact into a few pages in this edition, so a fat volume on this champion gag man will soon see the light of print, enveloped in as many writing samples as I have the strength to type out.

Thanks also go to the entire Ameche clan, Tim Brooks & Earle Marsh (for authoring *The Complete Directory to Prime Time Network and Cable*

TV Shows), Kelly Buttermore at The Museum of Television and Radio, Suzanne Gronemeyer, Tom Heathwood, Marsha Hunt, Jane Kean, Alex McNeil and his *Total Television*, Brian & Joel Rapp, Charles Stumpf and Rebecca Varner for their help with tying up all dangling loose ends. And a very special thanks to Laura Wagner for all her great and inspired writing and editing on this book.

There are some who might say the story ends with the Bickersons' last *new* appearance—that of the commercials they did in the 1970s. But considering the fact that many people reading this, including myself, got their first taste of the duo by way of officially re-released tapes and the infamous mp3 controversy, I believe the story actually continues to this day, and beyond.

Perhaps the Bickersons are not the most popular radio team around, since they only briefly had a whole half-hour series to themselves once, and perhaps the repetition of the routines kept it from progressing as far as it could, but for sheer laugh count, it must be an impossibility to beat Don Ameche and Frances Langford as John and Blanche Bickerson in The Honeymoon Is Over…

– Ben Ohmart
February 2004

John and Blanche Bickerson

Blanche
wears a beautiful Evans sharkskin handbag trimmed with snakeskin, with calfskin shoes.
has dizzy spells every five minutes that last half an hour.
wears glasses and is minus a couple of teeth.

Blanche Bickerson, quarrel-monger extraordinaire, was a complex woman. She longed to be treated like a frail, loving girl, and wasn't afraid to yell like a scream queen to get it. Not much is known about her early life, but she did have the distinction of having been voted Ms. Clam Harbor Lighthouse of 1931. Her first job in life had been as a school teacher, where she began to develop an ultra-strong constitution: she'd already had measles, the flu, mumps, and always came back stronger. But she had no resistance to John Bickerson whom she met before she had any sense. Years later, she claimed that she had more boyfriends than anyone in her circle; she could've married any six men, but married John for spite. John naturally asked, "What did you have to spite *me* for?" She had a little money, but John later insisted that wasn't why he married her. "I wouldn't marry you again for all the money in the world!"

By age 36 (or 28 by Blanche's count) John had bought her a home beauty kit for her birthday, but she refused to use it, citing that no one would use it but a homely woman. John admitted that the salesgirl from whom he bought it uses it, and she's not half as homely as Blanche. The next year he got her a genuine alligator traveling bag, engraved with her name. Two years previous, he bought her a set of encyclopedias. "It's not hard to see what you're thinking," she said. "I'm stupid, I'm ugly and you want to get rid of me." Her contradictory attitude at any given moment made it so that John could never win. Once he'd saved up enough money, he wanted to send Blanche on a round the world cruise. But the first thing she said upon receiving such a compliment was, "Suppose I don't want to go there. Suppose I want to go someplace else."

Always beefing, one of her favorite topics of complaint was the amount of work she had to endure at home while John was out scrounging a living. Oh yes, she had a maid once, but she wasn't with them long. As John admitted, "She was *never* with us, she was against us from the start!" She swept (everything) behind the door, but more than likely could not stand Blanche's overbearing personality, and left. Blanche would usually have to get up at 7 to make breakfast for John, then wash the dishes, sweep the floor, make the beds, do the shopping, do the laundry. John never offered to help. It rankled Blanche to no end that their friend Mel Shaw was always making up the beds with his wife, or washing the dishes with her, or mopping up the floor with her.

Whoever told Blanche she was a competent homemaker was an idiot's stupid brother. She insisted on darning John's socks, constructing new underwear for him out of her old bloomers and making him shirts without shirt tales. If John would complain about the latter, Blanche would simply bellow that he should wear his pants higher. "I can't wear them any higher," he complained. "I wear them so high now I have to unzip them to blow my nose!"

Eating Blanche's creations was an individual experience. The first stew she ever made for John, the cat ate before he had a chance to sample it. But he did get her a new cat. (Actually, according to Blanche, drinking bourbon did the poor thing in a month later; the silly feline mixed it with milk though John *begged* her to drink it straight.) For dessert, Blanche didn't believe in making pies with crusts, but the paper plates were chewy enough.

To be fair, sometimes John could be a difficult man to cook for. Once, he went on a two-month binge and refused to eat nothing but pig's knuckles, and Blanche had to work her fingers to the bone providing them. He also preferred duck eggs to the chicken variety. Of course with this kind of incentive, and a deformed sense of cookery she inherited from her mother, Blanche's choice of foods was prodigious.

THE BLANCHE BICKERSON MENU
For Breakfast – Your Choice of:
Onion Soup (in place of coffee)
Chowmein
Meatballs and Spaghetti
Deviled Oatmeal (contains a whole avacado and
three bunches of green onions)
Popcorn and Sour Cream

For Lunch & Dinner – Your Choice of:
Stewed Rabbit
Encheladas
Creamed Anchovies
Squid (stuffed with kelp leaves and goat's cheese)

Plus a Choice of Exotic Desserts:
Curried Tapioca
Orange Meringue Brocolli Dreamcake
Cake (includes mustard greens, two fish heads, a
pound of chicken gizzards, and cotton seed oil)

At one point, she admitted the only things she could cook were (rubber heel-looking) liver and rice pudding, though it was hard to tell them apart. One of her favorite desserts to attempt was a two-foot long rhubarb pie, which was chock full of vitamins, when you don't bother to cut or clean the vegetable first. She was always thinking up little ways of enticing John to love her more with her cooking. She once bought a real turkey for John to murder for Thanksgiving, tying the poor thing down on John's bed.

But as crazily as she experimented, she was determined that her man should never go hungry. Even when leaving for a few days, she'd make sure there was a bathtub full of rice; John would never touch it, rice being connected to one of the saddest occasions in his life.

Blanche's biggest problem was definitely her selfishness. She didn't mind seeing John off to work looking like something out of Oliver Twist, but she also thought nothing of spending $1,200 they didn't have on a bald mink coat. Or a plucked skunk. John was bitter about the whole incident. "The mink stinks and the skunk shrunk!" She once spent $24 (wholesale) on a half-ounce bottle of perfume called *Perhaps*. "For $24," ranted John, "they should give you *Positively*!"

She did once try to *make* them some money, by buying $90 worth of Christmas cards, *all* of which stated:

SEASON'S GREETINGS

> Christmas comes but once a year
> And so let's hoist our cup o' cheer.
> I hope that you'll hear soon from Santy.
> Merry Christmas, dearest Aunty.

She was a strong, intelligent woman who was ill-used by her family, and could quip meaner than a Bob Hope writer. Blanche's overpowering nature was fueled by John's constant lethargy. If they'd had more waking hours together, surely he would've fought back more and put Blanche in her place, which, at times, was evidently just what she wanted from a husband. But by necessity, she was forced into playing the heavy.

Still, she was deeply in love with John, and only wanted attention, doing *whatever* it took to get it. To keep "beautiful" Blanche underwent a nightly beauty treatment (around one in the morning). She creamed her elbows, sprayed her chin, rolled her neck and endured a grease pack, guaranteed to make her beautiful in five treatments. Down to the wire on the fourth treatment, John knew that that fifth one must be a *pip*. The tortures that woman went through on her quest to look plain...a whole day under a permanent wave machine, and having her eyebrows professionally plucked to offset her eyes and improve the lines in her face. All of this was wasted on John who firmly asserted that "your eyes are offset enough, and you have plenty of lines in your face." And he preferred her eyebrows as is: nice and *bushy*. She'd also slip on false eyelashes to bring out her eyes, but the hubby was perfectly satisfied with the way they bulged already. A rat in her hair and shoulder pads completed the build-up.

John

has great legs (according to Blanche).
is allergic to dog hair.
has a dimpled hula girl tattooed on his stomach (the dimple was there before she was).
is as healthy as a horse, and works like one, though he does have neuritis in his leg.

John Bickerson was the everyman who got nowhere. His eyes drooped, his personality clashed, and the sleepier he became, the funnier he got.

His pauper's ensemble was atrocious. The zipper kept coming off his pants. To keep body and soul together, he made due with do-it-yourself creations: he cut the straps off Blanche's old garter belts and wore them for bow ties, had all his teeth knocked out to save on eating, sewed heels on her old pocketbooks and used them for shoes, had his feet half-souled in a blacksmith just to save on shoes, cut down her old girdles and wore them for suspenders, sewed collars on his underwear to save on shirts, didn't take the bus but slapped a number on his shirt and galloped to work as a marathon runner, threw himself out of his office window once just to get a free ride home in the ambulance, cut his own hair, used his tie for a belt, nailed rubber heels on his socks for shoes, hocked his fillings to pay the dentist bill, had his feet painted black to save on shoes, and Blanche used his best shirt to drape around the canary's cage (the poor bird was sensitive to light).

He was also the only man in the world with one slipper, which he would pack away and take on and off whenever Blanche coaxed him into getting her a sleeping pill or glass of water. Sometimes he'd hide it under the bed. "I've only got one and I have to protect it with my life." He won it in a raffle on a shared ticket; that's just how much Fate hated him. John had just the one suit, which he kept painting different colors to fool people; he looked like an Easter egg when it rained.

How much of it was true is hard to say. When he began ranting that he doesn't *drink* his bourbon anymore, but licks the label and sticks his nose in a light socket, it's clear he's pushed the envelope too far. "I just chew the cork and hit myself over the head with the bottle!"

Blanche would starch the bottom of John's socks and make underwear for him that ended up looking like parachutes and lace curtains. She made him a sweater out of old slacks, making Bickerson the only man in town with a V-neck seat.

The wife claimed he wasted his money on things they never use… like the fire extinguisher and his life insurance.

John sold bowling balls (though Blanche kept assuming they were billiard balls, for some reason) door-to-door, but she made him quit, embarrassed to tell her friends what he did for a living. "It sounded as though I was trying to start a fight." So, he detoured into the elegant employment of pitching vaccuum cleaners door-to-door. It was better than his first job as a married man: a mattress filler (Blanche was pretty sure he'd been a *waitress feeler*), stuffing mattresses with something called Kapok!

John put in incredible ten-hour days, sometimes more for the overtime. Often the exhaustion was so much, he'd come home and fall into bed with his shoes on. "I work like a horse, I might as well sleep like one." John was not a lucky worker. He was once given two weeks vacation with pay the same day his employer filed for bankrupcy, and had to send the check back.

Every morning of his life he took his lunch to work. Unfortunately, Blanche hadn't fixed him a lunch in years. That stuff wrapped in brown paper was the garbage.

The poor guy's major sin and ultimate instigator of most of his arguments with Blanche, was his whining, rasping, growling, giggling, roaring snoring. John was completely oblivious to *everything* when he was out like a light, and what a time he had. It was the only time he was at peace with the world. Alas, Blanche could not stand his foghorn imitation.

The evil of the situation was that Bickerson had a long uvula which flattered against his palate, according to that quack, Dr. Hersey. The doc could cure it with a very simple operation, but John just didn't trust the hack. "I don't care if he knocks it off with a hockey stick! Nobody is going to lay a hand on my uvula."

Blanche compared the unearthly sounds to sleeping with an outboard motor, *The Thing from Another World*, a pinball machine and a jet plane. But his affliction had many names:

1. Grunter's Disease
2. "A rare form of insomnia that prevents *others* from sleeping"
3. Contagious Insomnia, or Schmo's Disease
4. "A rare form of insomnia that keeps the patient in a complete state of lethargy for 8 hours at a time."
5. Intermitin Insomnia or Woodchopper's Syndrome
6. Cyclode Insomnia or Blaster's Reaction
7. Undulant Insomnia or Blaster's Reflex
8. Oxfell's Syndrome
9. Progressive Insomnia or Parklay's Syndrome (a condition that makes the patient wake up once every two or three days)
10. Raucous Insomnia or Whimper's Malady
11. Induced Insomnia or Jabbering's Reaction

Blanche tried everything to cure him; taping up his mouth with cort plaster, then his nose, didn't help. Obviously, he snored through his pores. Even the persistant dripping of water will eventually wear away a stone—so, finally John succumbed to Blanche's many years of hammering on him to have it cured. The hospital operation was to take only 15 minutes and was completely safe—and expensive. Dr. Hersey wanted $200 down plus $25 a month for 11 months, plus charges for extras; he was buying a new car at the time. The operation was $10 cheaper without the anesthetic, which was tempting to Blanche, but she ultimately decided that if John didn't snore, they wouldn't be up all night talking, which was the only time they had to be together. So she decided against it.

For a second opinion, Dr. Marvin said that John had a deviated septum. His operation required

> **Snoring**
> Snoring occurs when throat muscles, open during consciousness, sag inward when relaxed. This forced breathing vibrates the uvula and soft palate when air is forced through the narrow air passageway on its way to the lungs.

> **UPPP**
> The preferred surgery to rid yourself of snoring is called Uvulopalatopharyngoplasty. It tightens the flabby tissues in the throat and palate, expanding air passages.

> **How To Cure Snoring**
> Lose weight
> Develop good muscle tone
> Sleep on your side
> Avoid alcohol!

chiseling, which John Bickerson understood well after seeing his bill. John had suggested Blanche see Dr. Marvin once before, when she thought she was at death's door. He knew the doctor would pull her through.

Then there was the snore specialist, Dr. Hugo Rasper, the head surgeon at a goat clinic in Salzberg. Among his most celebrated patients were the late Lord Martin, the late Charles Canterberry, and the late Countess Fong. His convenient payment plan worked out that you're completely healed the day you make your last payment. At Park Haven Hospital, he told Mrs. Bickerson that John was a mouth breather suffering from Clinefeld Sterder, a respiratory disorder resulting from a post-pherengel condition. Just a stitch in his palate to shorten his uvula and he would be cured. But it never happened.

John had no idea he snored (like most people), but claimed he was also a light sleeper, often kept awake when traveling by "some fat guy" snoring in the next room. Blanche knew better. To prove the man's indestructableness she said, "About an hour ago we had the worst thunderstorm ever and you never even budged." John was indignant. "Well, why didn't you wake me. You *know* I can't sleep when it's thundering."

"You wouldn't wake up if we had Big Ben in the room."

"Big Ben who?"

> **Uvula**
> According to Webster, the uvula is "the pendent fleshy lobe in the middle of the posterior border of the soft palate." The palate is the roof of the mouth which separates the mouth from the nasal cavity.

John may not have known his own body, but that didn't stop him from trying to cure his wife at times. Little did he realize she faked most illnesses just for the sympathy. To aid his wife in her ailments, John would often suggest insane family remedies. For a stiff neck or a sprained ankle, rubbing on chicken fat was the best. A stomach ache, the man claimed, was best soothed with hot ginger ale and oatmeal: "Make a new man of you." Fried cucumbers and hot root beer was also supposed to do the trick. He used it as a poultice, to draw the pain out. Bourbon, of course, was the mainstay to a healthy body, according to John, which could cure more ailments than death. But Blanche often complained, "If you treat me for indigestion, I'll probably die of liver failure."

"Listen," shouted John, "if I treat you for indigestion, you'll *die* of indigestion!" A bourbon-soaked mustard plaster was good for stomach pains, if you scrape the mustard off first; you hold it over your face and squeeze it.

John's only discernable hobby seemed to be working on his 1932 Essex during his once a year two-week lull from slavery. He would disappear under it with Nature Boy (wiping his hands on that cat's golden coat), and try to tune out Blanche's consistent nagging that he should stop wasting money on fancy car accessories (like a new windshield wiper and crank handle) and go collect his unemployment insurance. At least he had time to paint the tires so the tubes wouldn't show.

The Marriage

"Before you married me you told me you were well off."
"I was but I didn't know it."

In their passive courtship days, John would hang around night after night bringing candy, flowers and heaven-knows-what-else to the petite Blanche who assured her groggy husband that she never ran after *him*. He made many promises to give her a mansion and twenty servants. She didn't investigate his bank account but did hire detectives to find out about his salary. She did everything she could to discourage him, including not accepting him the first time he proposed (mainly because she wasn't there). They eloped and were married by a Justice of the Peace (not the Secretary of War, as John would have it).

"You stopped loving me the day you married me."
"That wasn't the day at all."

Only years after they were married did Blanche admit that her mother pleaded and pleaded with her not to marry "that man." On learning this, John, with a tear in his eye, finally realized how long he'd misjudged that woman.

Once hitched in 1942, romance wound down quickly. True, John would offer his mate half the newspaper at breakfast, and would slow the car down when picking her up to go somewhere. But they lived in a crummy New York City apartment and slept in separate beds. To raise enough money to afford a house, John briefly took a second job as a streetcar conductor. Blanche tried to help by sending all her friends to ride on his car, thinking he'd get to keep all the nickel fares. This was during his seven-year stint as a dog food salesman.

Blanche sneakily attempted the same thing, securing them a *very* nice apartment at a much lower rent than they were paying. The only thing she neglected to tell her husband was that he was required to get up at four every morning to bank the furnace. It was just one of many duties he'd have to perform as janitor of the building. Bickerson revolted, and they went back to live in squalor.

"I don't think. I know."
"I don't think you know, either."

Unfortunately, their wedding anniversary usually fell on rent day, cheering down John no end. On their eighth, Blanche was hungry for something special. "We've been married eight years. Don't you wanna do anything?" "No," said John, "it's too late to do anything." Yet, Blanche did throw a party for her crumb friends which John missed because of another full day's work. He did peel all the potatoes the night before the party, though, and bought Blanche an old beach bathrobe for $8. That was upsetting. "$8? A dollar a year for washing your shirts, cooking your meals, darning your socks, raising your children?" "We haven't got any children." "Well, what do you want for a dollar a year?!"

They never had kids, which was a good thing, probably. John hated children anyway, "because I can't bear them." They considered adopting once: a little girl, which Blanche insisted on so she could shop for her, teach her everything she knows, so that John would come home to find *two* Blanches, ultimately. With a threat like that, no wonder the plans fell through. It would have been no life for a child. Besides, Blanche once admitted, "I'm satisfied just to be with you." To which John replied, "Well, you're in better company than I am."

In place of that, Blanche did once get a puppy from the pet store, even though John was allergic to dog hair (it played up his sinuses, making him snore like a bilge pump). That didn't stop her from putting the little "beast" in his shirt drawer.

"You're a fine one to talk about matrimony. You don't even know the meaning of the word."
"It's not a word, it's a sentence."

Still, there was enough love between them to keep them together for a lot of years. To try to rekindle the flame, they once took a plane to Niagara Falls, though the trip was doomed from the start—the cat gets airsick and the canary is afraid of flying. But the trip was cancelled when Blanche spent the airfare on a sheared beaver coat; actually, the airfare money replaced John's insurance money which he kept in the sugar bowl. But Blanche made up for that: she wrote the company advising them to deduct his current premium from the money they'll owe her when John drops dead. A third honeymoon had them driving to a hotel at Niagara, but Blanche was so pushy, she made sleepy John carry all the luggage up to their room when they arrived after midnight, plus unpack everything: drawers in the dresser and dresses in the drawers.

To elicit love and sympathy from the overworked husband, Blanche once feigned a sprained ankle, which John lovingly (or as near to it as he could get) administered with chicken fat. She could still walk around, but kept hitting her ankle with a heavy spoon whenever the black-and-blue marks started to fade.

"And to think you used to kiss me every time I turned around."
"I never *kissed you when you turned around."*

Blanche's irrationality stemmed from John's never being home, so she devised clever or weird ploys to keep him talking the hours, as late as they were, he was home. When she claimed that he was only tantalizing her and thinking of himself by having his life insured for $10,000, John promised to drop dead in the morning. "You say it, but you won't do it!"

In every "loving" marriage there is a green-eyed monster; in this case, it came in the guise of a curvy blonde named Gloria Gooseby. Whatever Gloria's *true* hair color might have been (Blanche was not convinced she wasn't a bottled blonde), she had the kind of body that could stop a truck. Blanche knew it was only her expensive clothes that bought her wholesale sex appeal. She was the only other woman in John's life; by default. He *hated* the sight of Gloria Gooseby and forbid his wife to ever mention her name. But Blanche just would not leave the woman alone, especially in times of stress; a combination of inferiority and jealousness kept Gloria "in bed" with the Bickersons for many a year.

"She has to struggle out of 12 pounds of cosmetics before you can even get close to her," yelled Blanche. John countered: "I always get close to her and she never struggles!"

"Gloria Gooseby may have a pretty face and a nice figure—but I've got brains, and after all, it's the little things that count."

How that monkey wrench named Gloria ever came to be in their lives is unclear, but she was as much a part of their marriage as lethargy. John would rave more than once: "I'd like to spend one night in this bedroom *without* Gloria Gooseby! Just one night!" Blanche was certain there was something going on between the two of them, especially the way John kept staring at her. "I don't stare at her," he said simply. "It's just that she wears those outlandish dresses and they bring out her eyes." "They bring out yours too," admitted Blanche. John had to assure his wife constantly that Gloria means even *less* to him than she does.

Gloria loved to wear strapless, backless gowns, but when Blanche wondered how she would look in one, John caught hell by musing, "Skinless and boneless."

"Tell the truth, John. If anything happened to me, would you marry again?"

"Never! Never *again!"*

Blanche was a jealous woman, and not just when Gloria swished around. Every letter or telegram that came in the mail for John, whether marked STRICTLY PERSONAL AND PRIVATE or not, somehow miraculously was steamed open over a cup of tea. Once, the missive in question contained a 1946 tax return for $76.50 (equaling two year's savings in that household), which Blanche foolishly spent on a beautiful Evans sharkskin handbag trimmed with snakeskin. John gave in (as he always did) and let her keep it, since he didn't have the strength to get her anything for their latest anniversary.

"It wouldn't hurt you to kiss me goodnight, you know."
"It hurts."

Blanche was the most insecure wife who ever lived, always egging her husband on to tell her loving messages of encouragement and romance—usually at two in the morning. But bleary-eyed compliments did not fall softly on her ears. Once, forced into coming up with something on the cuff, John sleepily intoned that when he looks into Blanche's eyes, time stands still. But she wasn't going for it. "That could also mean I have a face that would stop a clock." When Blanche asked him to swear that he'll love her as long as he lives, he naturally complied, "Cross my heart and hope to die!" She wondered at the double-meaning of that, but John assured her he only meant it *one* way.

"Whatever happened to your get up and go?"
"It got up and went."

They didn't go on many trips. There was that time they were part of the wedding party on a fishing scowl. Blanche got seasick in the hammock she shared with a 55-pound white sea bass that had been dead for 11 hours, while John struggled on snoring in the one-mattress bed. All was well until John discovered that his wife had put his 8 bottles of liniments (read: bourbon) in the wall safe (porthole). "I wondered why that school of sardines was chasing that shark!"

They did manage to get away a few times. They once went 400 miles to a hotel in San Francisco (obviously, they were living in California at the time). The Presidential Suite! Naturally, they got there at two in the morning. Things were not ideal at first—every room was full up with a convention of glassblowers. None of them blew, but the Presidential Suite was free until six in the morning, at which point they had to scram.

They also once took a house trailer to Yellowstone National Park—or at least part of the way. They drove steadily for nine hours, then had their car stolen after going into the trailer for a sleepy battle. Thinking quickly, Blanche managed to copy down the thief's license plate number.

"You know I love you so."
"So what?"
"That's what I say, the hell with it!"

The bickering stopped once—at Christmas. In a rare moment of generosity on both their parts, love won the day. Blanche sold her mink (which she bought for John's birthday) to buy him a portable bar which he proceeded to shower with kisses. But that same hollerday John sold all his bourbon to purchase her a genuine plucked-skunk muff ("that could hold two quarts"), custom-made to go with her fur coat. It was a touching Christmas, much like the famous O. Henry story, ended by John's eating the white liver she made for him with love.

"Would you miss me if I ran away?"
"Sure."
"How much would you miss me?"
"How far you running?"

The Cat

Nature Boy, a demon from hell in John's eyes, was one of the few cats allergic to fish, but could go an entire night in the refrigerator without freezing to death. When John occasionally offered some of his eclectic breakfast to the little beast, Blanche would simply scold, "You hate that cat, don't you?"

But she loved him. She was once going to enter the golden-coated creature in a cat show. Neither Bickerson thought he'd win, but Blanche knew he'd meet a lot of nice cats that way. No. Nature Boy was destined to remain a bachelor—probably part of the reason John jealously hated him with a passion. That cat could be just too savage sometimes, sounding like a cross between a wildcat and a runaway jeep. Luckily, a little dish of Coffee Rich sometimes lowered the growl to a meow.

Their first cat, Shiners, committed suicide after John found him drinking his bourbon. The truth was: he got his neck caught in a ball of string which John was loosening when Blanche walked in. Their other cat, Tonsils, also committed suicide after John caught him in the liquor cabinet.

Another of their cats, the blandly named Peter, whose mother was a champion Boxer, had kittens; Blanche never realized she was a female, so she kept John up one long night to think of a name for her. "Wake up, John, I've thought of a good name." "Go to sleep, I've thought of a bad one."

⌊ Nature Boy ⌋

"Nature Boy" was a song written by Eden Ahbez in 1948. The mystical flavor of the tune and lyrics of it have kept it in vogue for over 60 years. It's been recorded by every singer from Ella Fitzgerald to Celine Dion; Nat King Cole to David Bowie.

Broken-Down Relatives

Blanche's brother Amos Badger was one of the blights of John's life in the early years of their marriage. True, he got John in on the ground floor of 500 shares of Kentucky Salt Peter Mines preferred stock, but it quickly went into the ground. It was the only stock in history to move from the Stock Market page to the Help Wanted section.

Amos always had some scheme, such as running for State Assemblyman wearing John's tuxedo (which contained a hundred dollar bill in the pocket; put there by John to get his boss a birthday present) when he spoke at the Garbageman's Ball. Blanche was susceptible to his grafting ways. He once gave her $5 driving lessons and, by an amazing bit of quick thinking, managed to hit a police car head-on, then took a wrench to one of the annoying officers who claimed cop cars have the right of way. John's new, never-out-of-the-garage car was the only casually, which poor Bickerson later picked up where it fell—on Hill Street, between 5th and 8th Avenues.

When Amos became a notary public, he tried to entice John to make out a will by making out his own will and leaving everything he had to John, but John didn't want her. Amos was eager for that two bucks per seal he made, so he told John the story of the rich old lady who didn't leave a will, but the family was now fighting over the $100,000 she'd left in the bustle of her wedding dress. John, unmoved, candidly stated, "That's a lot of money to leave behind."

Unfortunately for John, Amos always came first in Blanche's life. When the deadbeat needed a suitcase on the night before John was to make an important business trip, she loaned it to Amos, claiming that John could easily put his suits in a paper bag. Amos even once convinced gullible Blanche to let him raffle off their apartment during the World War II housing shortage. Naturally, her brother drew the ticket and won it himself. Only John's yelling squelched the incident.

Still, John thought enough of the chiseler to give him a word of advice when the poor slob was considering getting married. *"Don't."*

Blanche's selfish sister Clara would borrow eggs from Blanche because they cost too much at the store—and tell her so. She was married to another grafter, Barney Dollop, a small man with the ability to eat twice his own weight in one sitting. Tomaine cooks ran in the family; Clara would also make outlandish dishes for her husband, like rudabega pudding and creamed calf's ears. They had a 14-year-old son which Blanche once had to bathe when staying with them for a week (and she didn't like doing it). Mrs. Bickerson would also have to wash all the dishes, sweep the floors and generally work like a slave (and sleep in the bathtub) while visiting. Clara didn't believe in saying thank you, but she did honor her with borrowing Blanche's unpaid-for mink coat for an afternoon at the movies.

Barney had been a court-martialed buck private, though he claimed to be a Field Marshall in the Army. John had his number. Any man who would lift Blanche's house key to have an extra made "for your own protection," was a schemer. He once tricked John and Blanche into staying with the Goosebys for two weeks (John's vacation) so he could use their house for a marathon poker game with members of the United Nations Pool Hall.

Clara and Barney once moved in for a week, subletting their own place to earn a little cash, forcing John to sleep in a cot in the kitchen. The first thing little Barney did upon unpacking a sandwich was attempt a long distance phone call to a barbershop (bookie) in Denver, then tried to take a shower. The entire shower unit came off in his hand; the plumber had just installed it—it hadn't even been screwed in yet. When chastised by Blanche, Clara tried to ingratiate herself by saying, "Let Barney do it. He's good at screwing things up."

The only thing Clara and John agreed on was that Dr. Hersey was a quack. The good doctor charged Clara $75 to deliver her little Ernie, but according to her, "Ernie was no $75 baby. The kid only weighed four-and-a-half pounds. That's more expensive than a rump roast."

It's hard to say just how many relatives Blanche had. There was Luke and Horty Pratt in Dutch Falls, Idaho who had 12 children (the last of which weighed 19 pounds, 8 ounces at birth). Then there was another sister in Peapatch, Maine. And not a saint in the bunch.

Uncle Raffy had no forehead and walked on his knuckles (actually, he was just a taffy-puller with very long arms). Once he became wealthy, he invited John and Blanche on a cruise after her cousin Eunice's wedding. But the great ship turned out to be a live bait boat, which charged the marriage party $4 a couple, BYOW (bring your own worms).

John did, however, ask daily about the state of Blanche's rich uncle Thermine's health. "The old goat" finally died in 1948, prompting the Bickersons to travel for the reading of the will. Even though she was his favorite niece, she didn't get a dime. Thinking she'd inherit all his money, Blanche quit for John, knowing it wouldn't look right for an heiress to be married to a bowling ball salesman. She also withdrew $200 out of their whopping $600 bank account to pay Arthur Murray for rumba lessons.

Eunice, with her lovely crew haircut, was hostess on Raffy's worm-ridden boat. The Bickersons also attended Blanche's sister Agnes' marriage to Willy, who showed up in baggy blue jeans, so John had to change clothes so he'd have a tux. Poor Agnes' eyebrows were so long she didn't need a veil. "The boy who married her got a prize," said Blanche. "What was the prize?" John asked. But they couldn't remain for the whole event, and finally crashed for the night at a motel. Blanche did not like that. "You've been to 50 weddings and always stayed for the ceremony. Did you ever regret it?" "Only once."

"Are you satisfied with our married life?
"Satisfied? I've had more than enough."

The Crumb Friends

"That idiot" Mel Shaw came to California around 1942 without a dime in his pocket, peddling sachets in a little basket door-to-door. He was an instant failure and still owes for the basket. He was one of the Bickersons' closest friends, which meant that John couldn't stand him, or his wife Louise.

The Sauce

To alleviate the stress of blissful married life, John Bickerson took sweet refuge in his membership to the Bottle of the Month Club, a Kentucky-based lifesaver. So necessary was this nectar to poor John, if Nature Boy tripped him up to make him break a bottle, the man would simply fume about his wet shirt, "I hope it's blood!" At least licking the remains off the floor was some solace.

> **Mel Shaw**
>
> The real Mel Shaw was an artist who worked for Disney on such classics as *Fantasia, The Jungle Book, Beauty and the Beast*, and was Phil Rapp's best friend.

The wife often complained about the vast amount of empty bourbon bottles that rolled around the house. Yet, he *had* to keep his dear dead friends near him. "I was with 'em when they passed away."

If Blanche was feeling particularly quarrelsome or sensitive and wanted to hear those three little words again, John would often take bourbon's name in vain and swear that he hopes he drowns in a pool of bourbon if he doesn't love her. More than Gloria Gooseby, she accused the real home wrecker as being bourbon. "You're in love with a bottle of bourbon. Go on—I can take it. Just give it to me straight." "It's better with soda," said John. She knew she was married to a great big corkscrew, an apt nominclature which John resented. He claimed that drinking is not one of his failures. "No," admitted Blanche, "it's one of your few successes." "I don't drink more than any six men you know!" John protested. He claimed he only drank because the doctor prescribed it for his snoring: a jigger of bourbon and two aspirin every night. It was just too bad that aspirin gave him a headache, so he was continually six months behind on the aspirin and two years ahead on the bourbon.

John once had a bourbon stain on his suit for months (in case there was liquor rationing, he didn't want to be caught short), and was outraged when the wife had it sent out to be cleaned. He also brushed his teeth with bourbon-flavored toothpaste and once sprained his ankle trying to get the last squeeze out of the tube. The dentist said he needed a stimulant for his gums. It turned his teeth pink, or, more aptly, bloodshot.

The Honeymoon Is Over: A History of The Bickersons

The mid-1940s was ripe for some marital tension in comedy. Burns and Allen, Ozzie and Harriet and later even Phil Harris and Alice Faye had their ups and downs and their share of crazy side streets down the highway of communal life, but when the half hour was up, radio audiences knew that husband and wife (often, and as in the above examples, *real* husband and wife) were blissfully happy. At least in the scripts. In those post-war years, but before the '50s firmly latched hold to the dark side of entertainment, audiences were content, but still eager for a change. They wanted more than a laugh; they wanted to connect with the characters. If they weren't quite yet ready for sheer realism, at the very least they were receptive towards a novelty that would take them away from the sweetness or typical situation comedy that was beginning to pave its way into early television.

So why did The Bickersons "work?" Sandra Loyer, a social worker and marital therapist with the University of Michigan Health Systems for 20 years, states:

"The Bickersons would present quite a challenge to a marital therapist today. In today's therapy offices we talk about marriage enhancement, nurturing, problem solving and conflict management, not necessarily qualities that are immediately obvious in the marriage of John and Blanche.

"John Gottman, PhD, author of *The Seven Principles for Making Marriage Work,* claims to be able to predict divorce after listening to a couple for just five minutes. He believes that happily married couples keep their negative thoughts and feelings about each other from overwhelming their positive ones. He calls this an emotionally healthy marriage.

"In *Fighting for Your Marriage,* by Markman, Stanley and Blumberg, they state that 'communication is the lifeblood of a good relationship…

however most couples have never learned to communicate well.' They developed the Speaker-Listener technique to teach couples how to communicate.

"If the Bickersons showed up in my office for marriage counseling, I would first wonder how they ever agreed on going to a therapist in the first place. Secondly, I would wonder what in their marriage they would want to change. After they talked about this for the first five minutes, employing Gottman's technique I would have to assume they were headed for divorce! I could then try to teach them how to implement the Speaker-Listener technique, but I'm not sure Blanche could stop complaining long enough to grasp the concept.

"Fortunately, for us, the listeners and fans of The Bickersons, we don't have to concern ourselves with whether their marriage will last or not—we know it did last and we are glad it did. I think that the key factor in the longevity of their marriage is that every night, no matter what, John returned home and Blanche was waiting for him. For all of us that was quite enough."

When Philip Rapp's humorous creation The Bickersons debuted on *Drene Time* in 1946, it was a truly original piece of business, even for its stars Don Ameche and Frances Langford who had never played this type of comedy before. Ameche had been cast in many film roles as the hot-headed editor and the take-charge film director, so he knew how to yell with the best of them. But for singer Frances Langford, who had until then only helped with some Bob Hope gags while touring with the comic, The Bickersons was a total departure from her on- and off-screen persona.

"Phil always said, 'Just play it like a nagging wife,'" recalled Frances years later. "And I would do it, and he would say, 'Nastier.' Actually, it wasn't hard to do at all. Phil's scripts were so well written that the laughs got themselves. And I got all that bad temper out of my system."

The characters of John and Blanche were the sole creations of Philip Rapp, one-time writer for Eddie Cantor and Fanny Brice, and currently employed writing films for Danny Kaye. Rapp often said that he based The Bickersons on his own marital strife, sometimes gleaning a few situations (such as the bagged garbage mistaken for lunch) from activities or notions his wife Mary might initiate. Phil and Mary, who met in their early vaudeville careers, remained married for over 60 years, however, never divorcing.

Drene Time regulars Danny Thomas, Frances Langford, Don Ameche performing for Wondervets Ben Saucier, Jim Scully at the Binmingham General Hospital in Van Nuys, CA. (*Photofest*)

Phil named the main characters after his brother John, once a comedy writer for Bob Hope, and John's wife Blanche. Other real-life names (Mel Shaw, Jon Hall) would crop up as characters or in-jokes within The Bickersons' 25-year career.

No one else ever wrote a line of The Bickersons—it was all and always Philip Rapp.

The Bickersons' theme song, "Please Go 'Way and Let Me Sleep" was originally called "Please Let Me Sleep" when it was first published in 1902. It was written by two songwriters who worked most of the time together: composer James T. Brymn (1881-1946) and lyricist Richard C. McPherson (1883-1944; sometimes writing as Cecil Mack), also responsible for turn-of-the-century hits "Good-morning, Carrie" (1901), "Those Tantalizing Eyes" (1902), "Zongo, My Congo Queen" (1904), and others. Its authorship is often attributed to the man who first published it, Harry von Tilzer. The moderate-tempo song was significantly slowed down for The Bickersons, always done as an instrumental, never disclosing the lyrics:

(*Brown University Library*)

(Verse)
I am twice as happy as a millionaire
Ev'ryday I have such lovely dreams
When I'm sleepin' money never gives me a care...
Trouble never troubles me it seems...

I don't mind no summer heat or wintry storm...
When I turn to bed I feel the spring...
'Larm clocks act on me just like a dose of chloroform.
When folks tries to wake me up I sing...

(*Brown University Library*)

(Chorus)
Please go 'way and let me sleep.
Don't disturb my slumber deep.
I would rather sleep than eat;
For sleep to me…is such a treat, treat, treat.

I never had a dream so nice.
Thought I was in Paradise.
Wakin' up makes me feel cheap.
So please let me sleep…sleep…

(Verse)
Ten o'clock this mornin' I was poundin' my ear.
Dreamin' I'm the warmest coon in town …
Landlord hollered, "Wake up quick an' get out of here …
Hurry up, the place is burning down!"

I got sore at bein' woke an' started to shout
"Stop that noise out there, for goodness sake ...
I can't watch no fire now, so you can put it out.
Burn your blamed old house when I'm awake!"

(Repeat Chorus)

Not the most politically correct song ever written, but popular in its day. Publisher von Tilzer gained much notoriety for the song by pretending to fall asleep and snore loudly during the verse, while it was being sung by minstrel singer Arthur Deming at the Chicago Opera House. Von Tilzer would then groggily sing the verse from his seat. Unfortunately, von Tilzer was too good an actor and if the ushers had not been let in on the secret, they would throw him out before his turn at singing. Once newspapers picked up the story, for years after, "Please Go 'Way and Let Me Sleep" underscored many a sleeping scene in vaudeville acts and some early films. Philip Rapp knew the song from his own theater days, and knew it was the perfect audio suggestion to grab hold of when plotting his Bickersons bit in the latter half of 1946.

Most reports put The Bickersons' origin as September 8, 1946 when the first *Drene Time* radio show aired over NBC Sunday nights at 10, sponsored by Drene Shampoo. But the first script using The Bickersons—indeed the first *Drene Time* script found in the Philip Rapp collection—was dated December 15, 1946, and obviously introduced the characters. John and Blanche were only minutely different from their regular components, the most significant changes being that The Bickersons had only been married for three years; that Blanche had at one time been a schoolteacher; and that John was more deviant in his quest for some serious sleep than he would later portray: he'd bought himself a double-thick sleep shade, lullaby musical pillow, toe mittens, electric pajamas and an automatic sheep counter. (The complete script is printed in *The Bickersons Scripts* book.)

Some accounts also mistakenly refer to The Bickersons' start coming on Edgar Bergen's show, whereas they would really appear on it two years later for a brief run.

With Marvin Miller announcing and Carmen Dragon leading the orchestra, *Drene Time*'s variety was classic. After the introduction of Don Ameche ("Blanche, why don'tcha let me sleep?) and Danny Thomas ("Progress? You call this progress? Kaiser is driving Fraiser around on a motorcycle!"), Frances Langford ("our glamorous Drene Girl") brightly pitches out the opening song, such as "The Best Things in Life are Free." Then, the obligatory commercial, tag-teamed between announcer and a pretty girl's voice: "Never before Drene could a shampoo reveal all the natural brilliance of your hair. Never before Drene could any shampoo leave your hair so lustrous, yet so easy to manage." Its creamy, whipcream lather was the secret to making your hair "easier to curl, easier to arrange right after shampooing. With hair conditioning action."

Ameche was the genial host for the evening. On radio, everyone was single. Don made a play for Frances after the opening commercial on the March 2, 1947 episode, but Franny had promised to sit with Danny Thomas while he was experimenting. Intro. Danny Thomas enters to applause. It's Spring, but Danny is having girl problems. No wonder, since his mind is filled with the stupid inventions in society. His new invention—a liquid beverage!—called Thomas Cola, which he then sings about. It'll make a 95-year-old feel like 94, and has an ebullient kerosene taste. The song continues through history, racking up celebrity endorsements for the vile stuff.

"Your hair can have that dazzling sheen," began the middle commercial, "the very first time that you use Drene." The ads lasted about a minute and were as repetitious as tickertape.

After Frances sings Carmen Dragon's beautiful arrangement of "Sonata," Marvin Miller announces the now-familiar: "Now here are Don Ameche and Frances Langford as John and Blanche Bickerson, with Danny Thomas as brother Amos, in The Honeymoon Is Over…"

BLANCHE: Close the window, it's cold outside.

JOHN: If I close the window will it be any warmer outside?"

Blanche complains of indigestion; she thinks that fish they had at the Goosebys' disagreed with her. "It wouldn't dare," emotes John. Blanche's main beef this week is John's having to leave for 24 hours for work. "What if a burglar comes in and finds me?" John: "It'll serve him right." She's concerned that absence will conquer John's love, but he *assures* her that the longer he's away the better he'll like her. To assuage her aching heart, Blanche requests $45 for a new hat to cherish while he's gone. "Look at Louise Shaw. Every time she's in the dumps, she buys a new dress." "I thought that's where she bought her clothes," ruminates John.

After a final goodbye from host Ameche and another long commercial, the show concluded.

The battling couple was a smash. In some quarters, from the public, network and sponsors alike, there was sheer outrage at the effrontery of these characters. Some called them crude, while others claimed they were simply unlikable. But Rapp and The Bickersons also had their champions.

In John Crosby's radio column, *Drene Time* was given high marks. After the changes of a new format and the introduction of several new characters, it was upgraded from its previous review, which called it "highly spiced hash." Now, "it's a very pleasant and comic half hour" with raves for everyone.

"I never thought I'd live to see the day when I'd call Don Ameche a good comedian, but he is; at least, on the radio he is." Danny Thomas was lauded for being "rough-and-tumble comedy of the Bert Lahr school."

"Miss Langford doesn't require much explanation unless you just arrived from Mars. She has a velvety voice, almost illicit in its femininity, and belongs to that exclusive circle of feminine singers who can be identified the moment they start singing. Incidentally, she appears to have conquered her former distressing habit of bursting into sobs, or what sounded like sobs, in the second chorus."

The old formula had Don singing, doing comedy, then tackling a dramatic spot, but now:

"The brightest spot on the *Drene* show is a skit between Miss Langford and Mr. Ameche. It's news to me that Miss Langford is a comedienne. She used to utter small comic remarks on the Bob Hope show but she was so overwhelmed by the bedlam that goes on over there that it didn't come off very well. In these small domestic comedies, she does very well.

"A recent skit concerned a woman who started discussing her husband's snoring and then, by a process of feminine irrelevance, proceeded to chatter on indefinitely about her looks, her health, her cooking, her husband's treatment of a child they haven't got, and, somehow or other, a $50 ticket on a racehorse.

"Though I scarcely believe the evidence of my own ears, it was character comedy with teeth in it; that is, it revealed a very unpleasant relationship between husband and wife and still was very funny. In the theater, it would be dismissed as a rather mild example of its kind but to find this sort of comedy on the air at all is a very heartening sign.

Phil Rapp, Frank Morgan and unknown man celebrate Frank's birthday.

"The advertising on this program, I'm afraid, is about as bad as it ever gets in radio. The name Drene is hammered into the listeners, by actual count, 29 times in half an hour. There ought to be a law."

The last week of January 1947 had stories running in all the columns that Rapp was to write a Bickersons play for Broadway with Ameche and Langford in the leads. The plan was for a summer tryout in the "strawhats circuits" when the radio show vacationed for the summer. Don Ameche was considering being in on the production end, perhaps producing or putting in money for the show, but nothing happened with the idea. Not then, anyway.

The new hit comedy team gained enough interest for the network to allow a half-hour pilot for a regular series to be recorded on December 13, 1947 entitled "The Pink Slip" with Ameche and Langford. But it was never picked up by a sponsor or aired.

When Drene dropped the show after a single season, CBS and Old Gold Cigarettes were quick to step in for another season. With the start of *The Old Gold Show*, a new format was called for, so Rapp adopted one that had worked so well before in his Baby Snooks years. Byplay between fibber Frank Morgan, Don Ameche, Carmen Dragon and sometimes a guest would make up the first half of the show, with The Bickersons comprising the latter. The guest would not be a Hollywood star, but an expert in the field of science, or an athlete (something odd like scuba diving), or a rank higher-up in the Armed Services, so that Morgan could weave his Baron Munchausen tales in and out of puns uneasily against the real authority of the week. Oddly, though Danny Thomas controlled the first half of *Drene Time*, Morgan was not given a role—ever—in a Bickersons spot. He was not even heard again once his bit was done; perhaps he had left the studio before the show was over.

Guests, especially stars, were not needed on the show, obviously, once Morgan got rolling into connoisseur mode. He could eclipse anything that came his way, as this complete script from May 7, 1948 distinctly demonstrates.

a Lennen & Mitchell *Radio Production*

Sponsor P. LORRILLAND CO. 308 N. Rodeo Drive
OLD GOLD SHOW Program
Beverly Hills, Calif.
Station CBS
Date May 7, 1948 Time 6:00-6:30PM Studio VINE ST.

Cast	Music Routine
FRANK MORGAN	OPENING THEME
DON AMECHE	"AFTER YOU'VE GONE"
FRANCES LANGFORD	MORGAN PLAYOFF
CARMEN DRAGON	"NATURE BOY"
FRANK GOSS	BICKERSON THEME
MARVIN MILLER	BICKERSON PLAYOFF
HITS AND A MISS	CLOSING THEME

WRITTEN AND DIRECTED BY PHIL RAPP

<u>REVISED</u>

MUSIC:	(ON CUE) OPENING FANFARE
MILLER:	(ON CUE) From Hollywood.
CHORUS:	(ON CUE) It's Old Gold Cigarette Time. If you want a treat instead of a treatment Smoke Old Golds. If you want a treat instead of a treatment Smoke Old Golds. We're tobacco men, not medicine men Pleasure is what we pack Oh, Old Gold cures just one thing The world's best tobacco! So, if you want a treat instead of a treatment If you want a treat instead of a treatment Smoke, smoke, smoke, smoke—smoke Old Gold. (PAUSE)
MILLER:	The treasure of 'em all, gives the most pleasure of 'em all.
MUSIC:	THEME (ESTABLISH AND FADE UNDER FOLLOWING)
MILLER:	This is Marvin Miller, ladies and gentlemen, speaking for the makers of Old Gold Cigarettes who are pleased to present the thirty-third in a series of new programs with Carmen Dragon and his orchestra, starring Metro-Goldwyn-Mayer's lovable Frank Morgan, the genial Don Ameche and charming Frances Langford, who sings—
MUSIC:	LANGFORD AND ORCH… "AFTER YOU'VE GONE"
CHORUS:	If you want a treat instead of a treatment Smoke Old Golds. If you want a treat instead of a treatment Smoke Old Golds.
MILLER:	Friends…we make no claims for Old Golds beyond this—for pleasure…for smooth, mellow, deep smoking pleasure…you can't do better than Old

Golds. Don't you see? We're tobacco men...not medicine men. We promise no cures, no treatments, no hocus-pocus. By golly...Old Gold cures just one thing...the world's choice tobaccos... to give you a milder...smoother, tastier cigarette. Yes...you owe it to yourself...to smoke a pack of these delightful cigarettes...Old Golds.

CHORUS: So...if you want a treat instead of a treatment
If you want a treat instead of a treatment
Smoke, Smoke, Smoke, Smoke
Smoke...Old Golds.

MILLER: Now here is your host for the evening, Don Ameche.

(APPLAUSE)

AMECHE: Thank you, ladies and gentlemen, and good evening.

DRAG: Pardon, Don—

AMECHE: Now Carmen, you promised—no more yockers.

DRAG: Oh, don't worry about that, Don. As far as I'm concerned this is Yockerless Friday. I just want to know what time it is.

AMECHE: It's five after six. Why?

DRAG: Don, would you think I'm an idiot if I told you something idiotic?

AMECHE: Er—yes. I think so.

DRAG: I thought so. In a few minutes I have to give the baby another bottle.

AMECHE: Baby!

LANG: Whose baby is it, Carmen?

DRAG: It's one of mine. My wife took the other kids to San Francisco yesterday, and she left the baby with me.

AMECHE: What did she do that for?

DRAG: Well, we had a nurse, but she quit this morning.

LANG: That's awful. Where's the child now, Carmen?

DRAG:	She's in my dressing room sleeping in a violin case.
AMECHE:	I never heard of such a thing. Do you know how to feed her, Carmen?
DRAG:	Not too well. That baby just won't eat a thing. I spent all afternoon tasting her milk to show her how nice it is—and now I don't feel so good.
AMECHE:	Want me to pick you up and burp you?
LANG:	Carmen, I think I'd better go in and see if I can't feed the baby.
DRAG:	Okay, but you better put an apron on. She kicks, and you're liable to get milk all over you.
AMECHE:	Frances, do you have any children?
LANG:	No.
AMECHE:	Well, you go ahead. I think I'll phone my wife and ask her advice about feeding. (RECEIVER UP…DIALS)
DRAG:	Ask her if she knows how to stop the kid from crying, too.
AMECHE:	(OVER DIALING) I will…Hello? Hello, Honey?…Listen, what kind of food do you give to a ten-month-old baby? What?…No, I'm not baby-sitting, I'm still on the air…Aren't you listening to the program tonight?…You're listening to what!?…No wonder we haven't got any Hooper…Listen, this is for Carmen's kid, he has to take care of it…Get some what?…Uh-huh. And how do you stop it from crying?…Yes. Yes. Thanks, Honey. Goodbye. (HANGS UP)
DRAG:	What did she say, Don?
AMECHE:	Carmen, your worries are over. Just give your baby an old watch or a ten-cent string of beads and she'll stop squawking.
MORG:	(COMING ON) That's what *he* says. I've given my baby a barrel of perfume and a mink coat and I still can't keep her quiet!

AMECHE: Frank!
(APPLAUSE)

MORG: Herman, you haven't been around very much. Where is this babe of yours?

DRAG: Resting in my dressing room.

MORG: Err—dressing room. Well, you've been around more than I thought. However, right now I'm interested in knowing whether any applicants turned up in answer to my ad in this morning's paper.

AMECHE: What ad?

MORG: This one. "Wanted – Serving Girl. Good salary. Must be willing and able." Dodger, I interviewed two hundred women and couldn't find one that was willing and able.

AMECHE: Why not?

MORG: Well, the ones that were able weren't willing, and the ones that were willing weren't able.

AMECHE: I see. Why are you so particular about a serving-girl, Frank?

MORG: Haven't I told you about the trouble we encountered with our present upstairs maid?

AMECHE: Your upstairs maid?

MORG: Yes. A self-effacing but rather beautiful young lady. I selected her from thirty applicants sent to me from the school for Wayward Girls.

AMECHE: Wayward girls! Aren't you afraid she might rob the house?

MORG: Oh, no. The trouble is I put her to work as an upstairs maid—but unfortunately we have no upstairs. She's been working for us for three months and I haven't told her yet.

AMECHE: You haven't told her yet? You mean you've been keeping the girl in the dark?

MORG: Every chance I get…(DOOR OPENS) The maid I'm looking for now must have—Well, this must be one of the applicants…Hello, my dear.

LANG: Why, hello.

MORG: Well! What a lovely chambermaid! I haven't seen anyone look so good in an apron since I was dispossessed at the YWCA. May I see your references?

LANG: I'm afraid I—

MORG: Never mind—I can see at a glance that you'll do. The job pays sixty dollars a month with board and two hundred a week if I'm not bored. Is that satisfactory?

LANG: Mr. Morgan, there must be—

MORG: You'll have a room overlooking the park—right under my room—and I promise not to overlook your room. Will you take the job?

LANG: I'm sorry, Mr. Morgan—but right now I've got my hands full with an infant. I have to warm a bottle—goodbye.

MORG: I didn't even get her name!

AMECHE: Are you a madman, Frank? That was Frances Langford, our featured singer, she's worked with you for months.

MORG: Oh…Frances Feetsinger. Works for Madman Muntz. Yes, well, she's a capable-looking girl, and it's a pity she won't work for me. Together we could have made a fine pair of domestics.

AMECHE: A fine pair of domestics?

MORG: Yes. She has such a sweeping figure and I'm such a handyman.
            (GIGGLES)

AMECHE: Do you really mean you didn't know that was Frances Langford?

MORG: Well, I thought she looked kind of familiar—but wasn't she wearing an apron?

DRAG: Yes, Frank, she's just helping me out.

AMECHE: He's got a baby in the dressing room.

MORG: A baby! Well, congratulations, Herman! Have a cigar.

AMECHE: It's not a new one! His nurse walked out this morning and Carmen's stuck with the baby. His wife's in San Francisco and she doesn't know about it.

MORG: Oh, his wife doesn't know she had a baby. Well, somebody better tell her—it's Mother's Day on Sunday.

AMECHE: Don't you understand, Morgan? Carmen needs somebody that knows about children. His kid has been crying all day and refuses to eat.

MORG: Refuses to eat? Well, the answer is simplicity itself, and it all dates back to the fathers' infancy. Herman—did your mother have any children?

DRAG: Just two—my brother and sister.

AMECHE: What's wrong with you, Carmen? Wait, aren't you one of the family?

DRAG: I guess so, but I was so small I didn't even count. You know, when I was born I only weighed a pound and a half.

MORG: Not really! Did you live?

DRAG: Sure—you ought to see me now.

AMECHE: Stop wasting time with Morgan, Carmen. You'd better get a doctor to look at your kid.

MORG: That won't be necessary, Herman. Long experience tells me that your child's difficulty lies in improper adjustment. By a series of simple test I can determine—

AMECHE: What are you giving out with, Morgan! Do you know anything about child psychology?

MORG: (LAUGHS) Are you serious, Dodger? Would you ask George Bernard Shaw if he knew anything about architecture?

AMECHE: But Shaw is a playwright.
MORG: He is? Then why should you ask him about architecture? My advice to you is to go to a good architect, tell him what kind of a house you want, and he'll—
AMECHE: I don't want a house! I want to hear what you know about child psychology.
MORG: Er—yes! Well, learning the fundamentals of child psychology is just like taking candy from a baby—in fact, the whole idea is to keep taking candy from babies. When you have more babies than you have candy, you divide them equally, add your age, take away the number you first thought of—and the answer is always nine. (Is there a page missing here?)
AMECHE: What's all that got to do with feeding Carmen's baby?
MORG: More than meets the eye, my boy. There are many reasons why a child becomes intractable and the best method of approach is to probe its ego and uncover its foibles.
DRAG: This is a girl.
MORG: That makes it more complicated. Girl babies are naturally more capricious and often manage to confound even the most discerning psychologist.
AMECHE: Frank—this isn't a problem child!
MORG: You never know. This may sound curious to you—but I was a problem child myself.
AMECHE: I can't believe it!
MORG: I was a trial to my nursemaid who understood nothing of psychology and made matters worse by dandling me on her knee. This led to some rather objectionable habits.
AMECHE: That's awful.

MORG: It wasn't so bad. The girl found she could pacify me by giving me frequent tepid baths and rapping me on the knuckles with a spiked club.

AMECHE: Sounds like an effective treatment.

MORG: Effective but temporary. The real trouble lay in my clothing.

AMECHE: Your clothing?

MORG: Definitely. Upon examination by the leading psychologist of the day they discovered that my behavior was due to a constriction caused by tight shoes, and without a moment's delay my parents procured for my pleasure some loose beauties. Booties!

AMECHE: And that made you normal.

MORG: It always has. But I was so impressed with the science of child psychology that I soon became a judge in Juvenile Court, where I had a chance to study the eccentricities of teenage girls.

AMECHE: Did you save any of these girls?

MORG: Well, I have one or two phone numbers left, but I threw away—oh! Save!—You mean did I reform them!

AMECHE: Yes.

MORG: Certainly, I wrote a mountain of books on the subject all published in every language known to—

AMECHE: What books?

MORG: Oh, all kinds. I received the—

AMECHE: What books did you write, Morgan?

MORG: Errr—write. Well, have you ever heard of the famous "Common Neuroses of Children?"

AMECHE: Yes.

MORG: Well, I —

AMECHE: You nothing! That was written by English and Pearson and published by Norton in 1929.

MORG: Err—English pub. Twenty-nine palms. Yes, well, when "Psychology of Adolescence" first hit the stands I—

AMECHE: You bought a copy because that was written by my father!

MORG: Your father! You know something about child psychology, Dodger?

AMECHE: Everything! The Ameches have been child psychologists for generations, beginning with my grandfather Wayward Ameche, down to Uncle Handcuffs and my Aunt Pistol.

MORG: Your Aunt Pistol?

AMECHE: A long-barrelled old bore. Always went off half-cocked when she was loaded.

MORG: What's going on here!

AMECHE: Plenty's going on, Morgan, and you can't get out of it.

MORG: Now see here, Dodger. I—

AMECHE: Go on! Nobody but a fathead would believe that you're a child psychologist.

MORG: Well, the world is full of fatheads. Thank heaven I see one now. Here comes that pleasant Mr. Lardbucket.

MILLER: I don't want to intrude, Don—but I don't believe Mr. Morgan, either.

MORG: What!

MILLER: I'm sorry, Mr. Morgan, but I'm tired of your jokes and I can no longer stomach being the butt.

MORG: Now let's stop twisting things around. I was only pulling your leg. Really, this is one time I need your help.

MILLER: (BORED) Mmmmmm.

MORG: Mr. Lardbucket, I don't want to bother you—

MILLER: Well, you do, you know!

MORG: What happened?

AMECHE: That settles it, Morgan. Not even Marvin believes you're a child psychologist. You might as well admit it.

MORG: Rubbish! If I had a baby here I could demonstrate—

AMECHE: Carmen's got a baby here.

MORG: Oh, I forgot. Well, I haven't tried the Morgan Method of feeding in a long time and—

AMECHE: Well, you're going to try it right now. Here's a vitamin capsule you can give her—if you can make her swallow it.

MORG: It would be simple to make the child swallow that capsule Dodger, if I just had my equipment here. Unfortunately—

AMECHE: What kind of equipment?

MORG: Well, for one thing, I need a hollow tube about nine inches long and half an inch in diameter. So we might as well wait for—

MILLER: Oh, no. I just happen to have such a tube in my pocket.

MORG: Oh, you would.

MILLER: It's my pea-shooter. I'd love to see how you give a baby a capsule with it.

MORG: It's very simple...Where's the baby?

AMECHE: Over here...(DOOR OPENS) Can we come in Carmen? Frank's going to give the baby her capsule with the Morgan Method.

DRAG: You're not gonna hurt her, are you, Frank?

MORG: Nonsense. Just stand aside, my boy...Hmmm... The child is wide awake. That makes it a little more difficult—but no matter.

DRAG: She's smiling at you, Frank.

MORG:	Oh, is that her face? Ill-favored little creature, isn't she?...Is this the one you couldn't get off the chandelier, Herman?
AMECHE:	Come on, Frank—quit stalling and give her the capsule.
MORG:	Yes...All right—now open wide—baby...There we are...Now, I'll just insert this evil smelling capsule in the tube like this—then I'll put one end in my mouth and one end in yours. Then all I do is blow gently.
DRAG:	Hey, that's pretty good!
AMECHE:	Well, go ahead and blow, Morgan.
MORG:	Here we go. (BIG BLOW SOUND) Ohhh! Help—quick get a doctor!
AMECHE:	What happened?
MORG:	The kid blew first! So long fellows, I gotta get a stomach pump!
MUSIC:	MORGAN PLAYOFF (APPLAUSE)
MUSIC:	INTRO..."NATURE BOY"
MILLER:	(OVER THEME) Frances Langford sings "Nature Boy."
MUSIC:	ORCH AND LANGFORD..."NATURE BOY" (APPLAUSE)
CHORUS:	If you want a treat instead of a treatment Smoke Old Golds If you want a treat instead of a treatment Smoke Old Golds
MILLER:	Folks...have you tried an Old Gold lately? Have you discovered what our choral group is so enthusiastic about? Well, listen...give yourself a treat—in the cigarette that can't be matched for smooth mildness and wonderful taste...Old Gold. Yes...Old Gold...truly...the treasure of 'em all...Old Gold...with a quality tobacco tradition

unmatched by any other cigarette. Because nearly two hundred years of fine tobacco experience and knowledge are in back of Old Gold. And to you, that means the mellowest, best-tasting tobacco found in a cigarette today. That's something real...something you taste and enjoy in every Old Gold. And that's the whole point...Listen...

2ND ANNCR: We're tobacco men—not medicine men. Old Gold cures just one thing...the world's best tobacco.

MILLER: Yes. Fine, choice, ripe tobaccos—that make Old Gold the tastiest cigarette you ever smoked. Tonight or tomorrow morning get a pack of Old Golds. Then, as you smoke them, compare the downright enjoyment an Old Gold gives you with anything else you ever smoked. Do—just—exactly—that, won't you?

CHORUS: So...If you want a treat instead of a treatment
If you want a treat instead of a treatment
Smoke, smoke, smoke, smoke
Smoke...Old Golds.

MILLER: Now here is Don Ameche and Frances Langford as John and Blanche Bickerson in "The Honeymoon is Over."

THEME: SOFT AND PLAINTIVE

MILLER: The Bickersons have retired. Mrs. Bickerson lies tense and un-relaxed in the darkness as poor husband John, victim of induced insomnia, or Jabbering's reaction, engages in another losing battle during an acute attack of the sleep-robbing ailment. Listen.

DON: (SNORES LUSTILY...WHINES...BROKEN RHYTHM SNORE FOLLOWED BY A BELL RINGING NOISE)

LANG: It's like being married to a pinball machine!

DON: (SNORES AND GIGGLES)

LANG:	That's been going on for three hours.
DON:	(SNORES AND GIGGLES MERRILY)
LANG:	John!
DON:	Mmm.
LANG:	Turn over on your side. Go on.
DON:	(A PROTESTING WHINE) Mmmmm!
LANG:	Wake up, wake up, wake up!
DON:	Wake up Blanche…Wassamatter…Wassamatter, Blanche?
LANG:	You've got to stop it, John! I can't lie here another minute and listen to those awful noises.
DON:	Awful.
LANG:	Why must I suffer all my life? You can stop that snoring if you want to—I know you can. No other man snores like you.
DON:	How do you know?
LANG:	I talk to my women friends. Their husbands are so quiet they have to keep waking them to see if they're dead.
DON:	Mmm.
LANG:	What I wouldn't give to be able to sleep thru the night just once!
DON:	Me too.
LANG:	Not to hear that snarling, and rasping and whining and roaring. Honest John, who else carries on like that?
DON:	Honest John.
LANG:	Very funny. Oh, you're so funny, John Bickerson!
DON:	I'm not funny, Blanche—I'm just sleepy.
LANG:	What about me? I haven't slept for so long I'm a nervous wreck. My face is full of lines—I'm losing my youth. You'll be sorry. When I've changed into a withered old crone, you won't like it so well.

DON: Oh, I do too.

LANG: What?

DON: I mean you'll never look like a withered old crone. You haven't changed since the day I married you. You look great.

LANG: That's not true. You're just trying to make me feel good.

DON: I am not!

LANG: You are too!

DON: I am not! I wouldn't make you feel good if it was the last thing I ever did!

LANG: How well I know it! Telling me I haven't changed since you married me. That's just a defense because you know you're to blame.

DON: Oh dear.

LANG: Go on—take a look at our wedding picture. It wouldn't hurt you to see how pretty I used to be.

DON: It hurts.

LANG: And the picture didn't do me justice, at that. We never should have paid that photographer.

DON: Beef, beef, beef.

LANG: I still don't see why you let him get away with it, John.

DON: Oh, go on. It's the best picture you ever took in your life and you know it!

LANG: How can you say that? Look at it—it's on the dresser. Go on—look at it.

DON: Not now.

LANG: The pose is all right but I've got my lips apart and I'm showing the end of my tongue.

DON: Let me see that. I didn't know there was an end to it.

LANG: It's all right for you to talk like that now, John Bickerson. But I might as well tell you—I'm not

	going to let you destroy my beauty!
DON:	Put out the lights.
LANG:	What a fool I am. For seven years I sacrifice every pleasure just to keep looking beautiful for you. I never wash the dishes so my hands will always look nice. I never clean the house so as not to get dust in my pores. I take taxis all the time—even when I go to the butcher shop—anything to stop my calves from growing big. Not once in seven years have I worried about our finances—just to keep from getting wrinkles! No woman suffers like I do!
DON:	Blanche, you've done enough for me! Starting tomorrow—I'll make the sacrifices.
LANG:	But John—
DON:	You can clean the house, wash the dishes, worry about the money and walk your feet off until your calves turn into cows! Let me suffer for a while!
LANG:	That's too bad about you! Why do you think I like to keep looking young and beautiful? Only to please you!
DON:	I'm pleased.
LANG:	If you wanted me to I'd even have my face lifted.
DON:	You don't have to have your face lifted.
LANG:	Really, John?
DON:	Really. I like it the way it is—nice and saggy.
LANG:	What kind of talk is that? What's the matter with my face?
DON:	Nothing's the matter with it!
LANG:	But you don't think it's beautiful.
DON:	Yes, I do.
LANG:	You do not.

DON: Oh, Blanche, I do.

LANG: Then why don't you say it!

DON: Blanche, you're beautiful! Your face is cameo-like in its perfection! Your nose is classic! Your eyes are like two limpid pools! Your lips are as luscious as ripe cherries—and I love you!

LANG: How can you love me—you never look at me!

DON: How can I look at you and love you? I mean, how can I look at you when I'm so sleepy. Please put out the lights, willya, Blanche?

LANG: No. You're not going back to sleep, John.

DON: Why not?

LANG: Because somebody has to sit up with the cat. You know as well as I do the vet said she's going to have her kittens any minute.

DON: Why do I have to sit up with the cat? That's her worry.

LANG: John, haven't you got any feelings at all?

DON: Listen, Blanche, I've got as much feeling as the next guy—but I have to get up in the morning and I can't spend the whole night playing midwife to an alley cat!

LANG: She's not an alley cat! She's got a pedigree as long as your arm.

DON: What pedigree!

LANG: The man at the pet shop told me. Her mother was a pure-bred Boxer.

DON: Boxer! A Boxer's a dog!

LANG: For your information, A Boxer is a cat, too. It's a special breed—they raise them in China. And our cat's mother was a champion Boxer!

DON: Well, she didn't know how to defend herself.

LANG: What?

DON: Her father was an ameteur fencer! Now stop talking about the cat and let's get some sleep.

LANG: I can't help talking. The poor little thing is in the kitchen all alone, friendless—nobody to worry about her.

DON: What's the matter with the goldfish and the canary? They're in there with her.

LANG: Oh, they don't even know what's happening.

DON: Maybe the goldfish doesn't—but the canary's pacing up and down in his cage.

LANG: John, please—I wish you'd go in and have a look at the cat.

DON: What for? I can't do anything. I wanna sleep.

LANG: She may have had the kittens already.

DON: Mmm.

LANG: Do you think so, John?

DON: Think what?

LANG: Do you think the cat's had the kittens already?

DON: No. She'll let us know when she has 'em.

LANG: How will she let us know?

DON: She'll drop us a litter. Goodnight, Blanche.

LANG: And to think all these years I didn't know she was a female. We can't call her Peter anymore. I'll have to think of a name for her. Why don't you help me, John.

DON: Mmm.
LANG: Let me see…Marie. No, that's no good. Louise? No, if I call her Louise, Mel will get sore. Gloria? No, the cat'll get sore…Hmmmm…Oh, I've got it! John! Wake up—I've thought of a good name!
DON: Go to sleep—I've thought of a bad one!
LANG: I'm going to call her Clara—after my sister. Isn't that good?
DON: Fine.
LANG: Clara's always liked her so much and she'll feel honored. And we can name the kittens after Clara's children.
DON: Kittens? Listen, Blanche—you don't think we're going to keep those kittens, do you?
LANG: Why not?
DON: Why not? Nobody keeps kittens. If you don't give 'em away or something you'll have nine million cats inside of a year! Who's gonna feed 'em?
LANG: Oh, they don't eat so much.
DON: How can you say that? That one cat alone can eat five pounds of liver and drinks a gallon of milk a week. That's more than I drink in a month!
LANG: You never drink milk!
DON: I don't eat liver, either. Nine million cats living in luxury and I don't even have the bare necessities of life.
LANG: What do you mean?
DON: Two weeks ago I ran out of bourbon toothpaste. Have I replaced it? No! This morning I sprained my ankle trying to get the last squeeze out of the tube!
LANG: You and that bourbon toothpaste! I don't know how you ever got that crazy druggist to make it up for you.

DON: The dentist said I needed a stimulant for my gums. And there's no better stimulant than bourbon.

LANG: It's turning your teeth all pink.

DON: My teeth are not pink—they're bloodshot! And the only reason I use that toothpaste is because you were always beefing about how many bottles I buy!

LANG: Well, people were beginning to talk.

DON: What do I care.

LANG: Well, I care! Do you think I like being married to a great big corkscrew? I don't get anything *I* want.

DON: All right, marry a cat doctor and have all the kittens you want! Now, I wish you'd put out the lights and let me get some rest.

LANG: Never a civil word—never a sign of affection. And that's the thanks I get for standing by you thru storm and strife—helping you up the ladder of success.

DON: Success?

LANG: Thank heaven we don't have children to see the misery their mother goes thru. I can just imagine if we had a daughter—a beautiful girl growing up into a beautiful woman—about to be married—and her famous father is gallivanting all over Europe—denying his family.

DON: Nobody's denying his family!

LANG: There she stands—a lovely vision in her bridal veil—no father to give her away—

DON: Blanche!

LANG: Why don't you come to your daughter's wedding, John!

DON: Why don't you stop blowing your cork! Nobody's getting married and I'm not famous!

LANG: But you'll admit I made you what you are today!

DON: I admit nothing. I'm a self-made man.

LANG: Well, that's the first time you ever took the blame for anything.

DON: Is that so? I'd just like to hear what you've done for me? You just said you don't do the housework, or wash the dishes.

LANG: Who cooks for you? I do! Who cleans for you? I do! Who does your laundry?

DON: The laundry.

LANG: Only once! And that was because the washing machine was broken. If it wasn't for me you wouldn't have a clean shirt.

DON: I haven't got a clean shirt.

LANG: You have too. I dusted one off yesterday.

DON: Dusted it off is right. And you pressed the collar with a curling iron. Besides, I wore it today.

LANG: Today? What happened to the shirt you wore Tuesday?

DON: I wore it Wednesday. And I was going to wear it again Saturday, but I spilled some gravy on it Friday, so I cut the stain out and made a brown collar for my Sunday shirt.

LANG: Oh, stop complaining. You've got two lovely shirts.

DON:	One shirt. And it's not lovely. It hasn't even got a shirt-tail.
LANG:	You don't need a shirt-tail. Just wear your pants higher.
DON:	I can't wear 'em any higher. I wear my pants so high now I have to unzip 'em to blow my nose.
LANG:	Oh, hush up and go to sleep.
DON:	Go to sleep, she tells me...Woman drives me crazy with cats and weddings...My brain is spinning...Now she says go to sleep. I'll—never—sleep—another wink—as long as I—(SNORES...PAUSE...PHONE RINGS)
LANG:	John!
DON:	Mmm.
LANG:	The telephone—answer it.
DON:	Hello.
LANG:	Go to the phone and answer it.
DON:	Oh...(STUMBLES OUT OF BED) Two o'clock in the morning and people call—(CRASHES INTO NIGHT TABLE) Owwwww! (RECEIVER UP) Hello!
MAN:	(FILTER) Hello. Is this the Bureau of Missing Persons?
DON:	Bureau of Missing Persons?
MAN:	I just found out that my wife ran away from home last month.
DON:	What?
MAN:	I say my wife ran away from home. She's four feet eight, weighs two hundred and seven pounds, and has mouse-colored eyes. I been kinda wondering what's happened to her. Have you got any word for me?
DON:	Yes.
MAN:	Well, what is it?

DON:	Congratulations! (HANGS UP) I never heard of such a thing! Man's wife ran away and he's looking for her...Must be nuts.
LANG:	Would you miss me if I ran away?
DON:	Sure.
LANG:	How much would you miss me?
DON:	How far are you running?
LANG:	I knew you wouldn't miss me. You're too selfish to miss anybody. And as long as you're out of bed go in the kitchen and see how the cat's doing.
DON:	Ohhh. All right, I'll see how the cat's doing... (DOOR OPENS)...Well, I'll be—
LANG:	What is it, John?
DON:	I can't believe my eyes!
LANG:	John! Don't keep me in suspense! What is it?
DON:	How could that happen!
LANG:	John—please! Tell me—has she had the kittens?
DON:	She had one kitten. The biggest, fattest kitten I ever saw in my life! Bigger than our cat!
LANG:	Let me see...(RUNNING FOOTSTEPS)
DON:	Look at that kitten, will you!
LANG:	Oh, you silly thing! That's not a kitten—it's her husband!
DON:	Oh—well, let him sit up and wait for this children. Goodnight, Blanche.
LANG:	Goodnight, John. (THEME...APPLAUSE) (CLOSING)
AMECHE:	Well, that puts the lid on the thirty-third program of our new series for Old Gold cigarettes, written and directed by Phil Rapp. We hope you'll be on hand next Friday night for Frank Morgan, Frances

	Langford, and Carmen Dragon and the orchestra. This is Don Ameche saying goodnight and good smoking with Old Gold. (APPLAUSE)
MUSIC:	THEME
MILLER:	Frank Morgan appeared through arrangement with Metro-Goldwyn-Mayer, producers of "Homecoming" starring Clark Gable and Lana Turner. Remember next Friday at Old Gold time it'll be Frank Morgan, Don Ameche, and Frances Langford with Carmen Dragon and his orchestra brought to you by P. Lorillard Company…a famous name in tobaccos for nearly two hundred years…makers of Old Gold Cigarettes…the treasure of 'em all…and listen…if you want a treat instead of a treatment…treat yourself to Old Golds…Buy 'em at your tobacco counters…Buy them in the cigarette vending machines. Don't forget every Friday night on CBS it's "Fun for the Family." Stay tuned for "The Adventures of Ozzie and Harriet" which follows immediately over most of these stations. This is Marvin Miller speaking.
	(APPLAUSE)
	THIS IS CBS…THE COLUMBIA…BROADCASTING SYSTEM.

"One of the things I always found interesting," recalled Joel Rapp, "was that Dad almost always gave the actors playing John and Blanche 'line readings.' He was absolutely adamant that the inflections, intensities, etc. be as he heard them in his head and didn't waste any time letting the actors find their own way. Don was the possible exception—he *knew* John Bickerson inside and out and was absolutely letter perfect in the way he played that role—and the snoring was all his, too—no dubbing, no snore-stand-in, all Don.

"I do remember a time when Lew Parker and Betty Kean made some sort of deal to do the sketches as part of their act, and by then they had done the darn thing so often, Dad didn't need to help them out. But at least once, I can't remember what city it was in, Dad made a point to go see their act to make sure they were doing it his way, which they were."

Time magazine thought Don and Frances were doing it right, calling The Bickering Bickersons "one of the sharpest skits on the air."

Success came swiftly, as did the inevitable litigation. On March 19, 1948, Phil Rapp answered a "complaint" issued by Addison Smith, plaintiff, denying the charges that he modeled his Bickersons after *Two Sleepy People* which Smith wrote and produced for radio over the Don Lee Broadcasting System. Rapp's lawyer requested they exchange scripts to see just what similarities there were. The suit was dropped when Smith failed to "state a cause of action," after Smith's attorney failed to render a legal opinion on the matter. Rapp not only proved his case well enough, but assumed the offensive by demanding that Smith no longer portray his characters in bed, which seemed to be the main issue at hand. A mutual agreement was signed by Smith and Rapp, which put the major onus on Smith to behave, with both parties releasing the other from plagiaristic liability. There was no cash settlement. The situation was closed.

In some ways 1948 proved to be Rapp's heyday. On April 20, he signed an agreement to write *The Inspector General* (working title: *Happy Times*), which starred Danny Kaye, and had a provision put in his Warner Brothers contract that he should have every Thursday, Friday and Saturday off in order to assume his writing/producing duties for *The Old Gold Show*. He received $2,500 a week for writing the film. In a year when the minimum wage was 40 cents an hour, the amount was staggering.

Obviously, he commanded a large salary, if rave reviews from John Crosby were anything to go by. In his May 25, 1948 *Radio in Review* column, Crosby acclaimed: "The air lanes are aquiver with the cooings of contented husbands and wives (Ozzie and Harriet, Phil and Alice, Ethel and Albert, to mention only a few), but there is one young couple who couldn't have been more thoroughly mismated and who make no bones about it. They are John and Blanche Bickerson, who are heard at the tail end of *The Old Gold Show* (CBS 9 p.m. EDT Fridays), and who are a sort of contemporary Jiggs and Maggie. On second thought, I withdraw the reference. Jiggs and Maggie aren't in the same league with The Bickersons.

"Blanche, played very capably by Frances Langford, is one of the monstrous shrews of all time. She makes her husband and Don Ameche take two jobs, a total of sixteen working hours, in order to bring in more money which she squanders on minks and the stock market. Meanwhile, he can't afford a pair of shoes and goes around with his feet painted black. In the few hours he has to sleep, she heckles him all night with the accusation that he doesn't love her. Her aim appears to be to drive her husband crazy and she succeeds very nicely. The harassed John's only weapon is insult, at which he's pretty good.

"Just how pretty Miss Langford contrives to transform herself so convincingly into this venomous witch is her own little secret. She nags with the whining persistence of a buzzsaw, a quality that can barely be suggested in print. Mr. Ameche responds in accents of tired loathing which could hardly be improved on, though they may well cost him the women's vote.

"At the risk of losing the women's vote myself, I'd like to go on record as saying I think The Bickersons very funny. In a medium which strives so desperately to spread sweetness and light, in which every wife is an angel of tolerant understanding and every husband dumb but lovable, the bickering Bickersons are a very refreshing venture in the opposite direction."

To this day, the definition of *Bickersons* equals Ameche and Langford in most minds. But there were exceptions. Joel Rapp remembered that "Frances took sick one day right before the program and Lurene Tuttle, a non-stop-working radio actress and good pal of Dad's, was doing a show right across the hall. Desperate for a last-minute replacement, he fetched Lurene who could play any part on radio (Sam Spade's sexy secretary, remember?) and she filled in for Frances that one night. Now, if that isn't a true story, it sure as hell is a good one—and I doubt if anybody can verify it either way."

The most famous early casting departure for the marital comedy team involved Rapp's loaning out his brainchildren for *The Charlie McCarthy Show* in 1948. On September 23, Rapp was given a contract for his Bickersons to appear on Edgar Bergen's series for 13 weeks, commencing October 3, 1948, at $1,500 per week, with options for 39 and 52 weeks more. Again, all rights remained with Rapp. But this time, though *The Hollywood Reporter* announced it would be Ameche and Langford, it would be Ameche and film actress Marsha Hunt.

Hunt could whine with the best of them, but when it came to building sheer terror in a husband, in comparison with the pugnacious Langford, she was just a little too "nice" for the role. Though the occasional new situation was created for the short Bergen run, most Bickersons scripts were word for word reprises of *Drene* and *Gold* dialogue:

(AFTER MIDDLE COMMERCIAL)

KEN: It's wonderful what the holiday season does to people, isn't it Edgar?

BERGEN: Most people, Ken.

KEN: Yes. I was just wondering how the Bickersons are going to enjoy their Christmas.

BERGEN: Judging from the way they spent it last year I imagine they'll be rather happy.

KEN: What do you mean?

BERGEN: Well, curiously enough, I ran into Bickerson shopping around for a present the other day and he told me all about it.

KEN: This should be interesting.

THEME: (SOFT AND PLAINTIVE)

BERGEN: Well, it was last Xmas eve and Mrs. Bickerson was busy wrapping presents in the bedroom, while her husband John, exhausted from the pre-holiday activity, put the (FADING) finishing touches to the tree standing proudly in the kitchen, the only other room in the Bickersons small apartment.

MAR: (CALLING) John!...John! Will you bring the scissors, please?...John! What's he doing in there? (OPENS DOOR)

DON: (SNORES LUSTILY AND WHINES)

MAR: How can a man fall asleep on a ladder?

DON: (SNORES AND GIGGLES MERRILY)

MAR: I'd better get him off of there. John!...John!

DON: Mmmmmm! (A CRASH AND A THUD AS HE FALLS OFF THE LADDER) Owww! Wassamatter, Blanche? What happened?

MAR: Oh, you poor dear. Did you hurt yourself?

DON: No. No. I'm all right. I wanna go to bed.

MAR: Oh, John! You never even touched your dinner. Not a morsel of it!

DON: I don't like the looks of it, Blanche.
MAR: Do you want me to warm it up for you?
DON: No. Just tell me what's on that big plate.
MAR: Are you trying to be funny, John?
DON: I'm not trying to be funny, Blanche. What is it?
MAR: You know very well I can only cook two things—liver and rice pudding!
DON: Well, which one is that?
MAR: How can you be so nasty on Christmas eve, John?
DON: Blanche, I just asked you a civil question, that's all. I didn't think it was liver because your liver always looks like rubber heels—but that stuff looks more like scrambled eggs so I thought it might be rice pudding.
MAR: Why don't you taste it and find out?
DON: I'm not hungry.
MAR: That's why you're always tired, John. You don't eat enough.
DON: I eat plenty.
MAR: What did you have for lunch today?
DON: You ought to know—you packed it for me. And listen, Blanche—I'm getting sick of carrying my lunch to the office in paper sacks. Why can't I go to a restaurant like the other—
MAR: John! What are you talking about? I haven't fixed your lunch for two years!
DON: Oh, Blanche! Every morning of my life I find my lunch wrapped in brown paper on the side of the sink!
MAR: Lunch! That's the garbage!
DON: Goodnight, Blanche.
MAR: Aren't you going to finish the tree?
DON: I can do it in the morning.

MAR: But, John—tomorrow morning is Christmas day. I expect a lot of people to drop in. The butcher is coming, and the milkman—
DON: Listen, Blanche—I can't afford to give those guys presents! Why did you invite them over?
MAR: I didn't invite them—they're coming to collect their bills.
DON: Bills? What bills? I gave you money for the bills.
MAR: Well, I had to buy presents, didn't I? My sister Clara sent me a package and I had to get her something in return.
DON: No, you didn't! Nobody asked her to send you anything!
MAR: Well, she did, just the same. So I bought her a bottle of perfume.
DON: How much was that?
MAR: Twenty-four dollars.
DON: Twenty-four dollars! Nobody can carry that much perfume!
MAR: It was only an ounce, silly. It's the latest perfume—very daring—it's called "Perhaps".
DON: Perhaps. For twenty-four dollars you should get "Positively"! Perhaps!
MAR: Don't be so crabby, John. We're not going to fight on Christmas eve—no matter what happens. Remember, you promised.
DON: Okay.
MAR: I'm not even going to get mad because you didn't send me a Christmas card.
DON: I did send you a Christmas card.

MAR: It isn't necessary to make excuses or alibis, John. I'm going to forget it entirely.

DON: I don't have to make excuses—I did send you a Christmas card! I mailed it five days ago!

MAR: Well, I hope you don't forget to send me one next year, too.

DON: Ohhh! What's the use!—All right—so I didn't send you a card.

MAR: That's all. Why didn't you admit it before.

DON: There was nothing to admit. I just said I didn't send it to end the argument—but really I sent it!

MAR: What did it say on it?

DON: It said "Merry Christmas to My Love"—

MAR: That could be anybody.

DON: Let me finish! It said "Merry Christmas to My Love, my wife, my life, my turtle dove—life with you is great it seems, I love you more than pork and beans."

MAR: You're only adding insult to injury, John.

DON: Well, how do I know what it said? I can't remember what—what's that laying on top of the newspaper? There it is! It's my card!

MAR: So it is! See? You didn't need to get excited after all. Thank you, darling—it's a lovely card.

DON: Wear it in good health. Well, let's open the presents and then go to sleep.

MAR: How could you, John! You know we never open the presents until Christmas morning. Besides, you haven't finished trimming the tree.

DON: All it needs is a string of lights. One of the bulbs is blown and that kills the whole string.

MAR: Can't you buy a bulb?

DON: The stores aren't open now. What time is it?

MAR: It's five past twelve.

DON: Good! It's Christmas Day—let's open the presents.

MAR: You didn't even hang up your stocking.

DON: I haven't got one that could hold anything. They look like lace curtains. Let's open the presents, Blanche. Come on.

MAR: Oh, all right.

DON: We haven't got very many this year, have we?... Who's this from?

MAR: That's from Leo Gooseby. It's amazing how you went to the one shaped like a bottle.

DON: Oh, is that what it is? (TEARS WRAPPING OFF) I hope it's good stuff...(PULLS OUT CORK AND TAKES A GLUG) Ahhh! Not bad at all.

MAR: John! That's shampoo!

DON: Shampoo! (TASTES) Why, that chiseller! Two-bit Leo! And to think I threw out thirty-nine cents on a tie for him!...What have you got there?

MAR: (OPENING PACKAGE) It's another present for you. From your boss.

DON: (EAGERLY) No kidding! Let me have that. Gee, it's a big one!

(TEARS PAPER OFF)

MAR: What is it, John?

DON: A five gallon can of lighter fluid. That's fine. Just what I need. I never heard of such presents.

MAR: Here's one from Edith Gordon.

DON: I'll bet that's a dilly.

MAR: (OPENING PACKAGE) Oh, Edith always sends something nice. Not expensive but it usually comes in handy. Well! Look at that!

DON: What is it?

MAR: It's a polo score pad! Isn't that nice!

DON: That'll sure come in handy. Honest, Blanche, you've got the weirdest collection of friends. Is

MAR:	there anything else?
MAR:	Just our presents to each other. Why don't you look at what I got you first. Then you can show me what you got for me. Close your eyes. I'll unveil it. (WHISKS OFF SHEET COVERING)
DON:	Well, all right. I hope you didn't spend to much, dear. I don't really want anything—
MAR:	Open your eyes.
DON:	(OVERWHELMED) Blanche!! Oh, Blanche, darling. It's beautiful! It's a dream! A portable bar! With a brass rail!
MAR:	Don't you think a kiss is in order, John?
DON:	A million kisses! (KISSES AWAY LIKE MAD)
MAR:	Well, stop kissing the bar! I meant a kiss for me!
DON:	I'm sorry, darling—it's too good to be true. (KISSES HER) You're wonderful. (WORRIED) Blanche—it must have cost a fortune.
MAR:	John—don't get angry—but I sold my fur coat.
DON:	(BLANKLY) You sold your fur coat?
MAR:	I wanted you to have the bar—and I didn't have the money.
DON:	(REALIZATION) You sold your coat! That beautiful fur coat that you bought yourself for my birthday? That gorgeous bald mink?
MAR:	I got seventy dollars for it. The bar cost eighty-five.
DON:	Oh, Blanche—you never should have sold that bald mink.
MAR:	It doesn't matter. I have a cloth coat—and I never get cold.
DON:	But you don't understand—open the present I got for you.
MAR:	(OPENING IT) I can't wait, John...Ohhhhhh! A muff! A fur muff.

DON:	Genuine plucked skunk! I had it made especially to match that coat. It can hold two full quarts. And you sold the coat!
MAR:	Well, what's the difference, darling! Someday you'll make a lot of money and then you'll be able to have a coat made to match the muff. I'm very happy, John.
DON:	I know, but—but—
MAR:	And you still have the gorgeous bar.
DON:	That's just it.
MAR:	What's the matter?
DON:	I sold all my bourbon to pay for the muff. That's great, isn't it? What a break for both of us.
MAR:	I think it's wonderful, John.
DON:	What do you mean, Blanche?
MAR:	I've never been so happy in my life. We both made a sacrifice and that's worth more than all the gold and precious jewels in the world. Just to know that you gave up a prized possession is proof enough that you love me.
DON:	I've always loved you, Blanche. I may holler and rant and act like a first-class crumb sometimes—but you never doubted that I loved you, did you?
MAR:	No, John.
DON:	It's been seven years, honey—most of it uphill. I haven't showered you with diamonds, or bought any yachts—but I try not to deny you anything. I suppose you have your little faults—what woman hasn't—or what man either, for that matter—we're both pretty sensitive people—maybe that's why we beef so much. Still, I don't think we're any worse than any other married couple. At least we have a safety valve and we can let off steam—some of the others carry it inside until the break comes. No, Blanche—I like it this

	way—and I love you more than anything on earth.
MAR:	(WITH A CATCH) John.
DON:	Hey cut that out! I'll prove how much I love you. Where's that liver or rice pudding or whatever it is you made?
MAR:	It's liver.
DON:	I'll eat every bit of it if it kills me! Let's go!
MAR:	(LAUGHING) Merry Christmas, darling.
DON:	Merry Christmas.
	(MUSIC...APPLAUSE)

Now that he knew The Bickersons could work with different actor combinations and that he could assemble good money for loan-outs, Rapp took more offers. He signed a contract with Elgin National Watch Company on October 18, 1948 to provide his Bickersons on their always-impressive Elgin Thanksgiving Day program for November 25th, at a price of $1,000.

Another Bickersons team was warming up in the wings around this time: singer Martha Stewart, and a name who would ultimately be forever synonymous with the name John Bickerson—Lew Parker.

"Lew Parker and I had an act together for about a year," recalled Martha Stewart, "and The Bickersons was the finale of our act. We had a bed with a headboard. It was the highlight of our act, it was so funny. The wife was constantly putting the husband down, and it really worked. We got a lot out of that stuff.

"The act was around 1948, after we'd made the film, *Are You With It?* I was under contract to 20th Century-Fox. They decided to let everyone in the musical field go—Vivian Blane, me, almost everyone. After the war, they did a few more musicals, and that was it. Lew and I had been friends for years, and we were both free. We hung out at Toot Shores', along with all the other acts. Toots was a great friend of Jackie Gleason's, and Lew's.

"Lew had had an act with someone else, so we got some material from that act, and added some of our own, getting someone to come in and write some special material. And then some popular things, and then The Bickersons. It had to be the late '40s, because then I went into *Guys and Dolls* in 1950.

```
                                                          -14-

MAR:    I can just imagine the mess you must have left in that
        kitchen.
DON:    No mess.
MAR:    Did you put out all the lights?
DON:    Yes.
MAR:    Is the porch door locked?
DON:    Mmm.
MAR:    What about the windows? (are closed?)
DON:    What about 'em?
MAR:    Are they closed?
DON:    Closed.
MAR:    Is everything shut up for the night?
DON:    That depends on you, Blanche. Everything else is.
MAR:    Oh, don't be so irritable. I never get a chance to talk
        (You can stand the sound of my voice, can't you?)
        to you during the day, do I? And when you come home
        from work at night, you're always so tired.
DON:    Mmm. (I can stand it fine.)
MAR:    How I envy those newlyweds that have the apartment next
        door. She's such a pretty little thing - and her husband
        telephones her fifty times a day. Why don't you do that,
        John?
DON:    I don't know her phone number.
MAR:    I mean, why don't you call me?
DON:    Call you what?
MAR:    (Yes you can!) You see? I talk and I talk and you never hear a word I
        say. You never listen to me.
DON:    Always listen.
MAR:    No, you don't! Your mind is always a million miles
        away....John.
```

Original script page from an Ameche-Hunt show.

"We worked nightclubs and hotels, in Atlanta, Georgia and Las Vegas. We could both sing and dance. We did 'That's Entertainment,' which is a good number. Then I got *Guys and Dolls* and Lew started going with Betty Kean, and they took the act that we did and they did it. It was good, she was funny. They had the act longer than we did. I had contributed to it financially. I saw them in Las Vegas and they were just sensational. The Bickersons was a big highlight of the show. People love that thing; they could bring it back today.

"Lew was a kind and loving man. Highly underrated. He could've gone much farther in his career, though he did an awful lot."

Lew Parker and Johnny Downs in *Are You With It?*

Dolores Gray and Lew Parker in *Are You With It?*

The Old Gold Show concluded on June 25, 1948, while the Ameche/Hunt collaboration on Bergen's series ended on his 500th show the day after Christmas of that year. According to one report on December 13, 1948, it looked as though The Bickersons would have another shot at a series all their own in 1948. Frances Langford, through the William Morris Agency, signed a year-long contract at $1,500 a week, to be raised every year the series continued. As usual, she was not to portray "any character similar to the character of Mrs. Bickerson" during the run of the contract, though she could perform "the part of a wife in any radio program in which you may engage with your husband, Jon Hall, provided it is not similar to the Mrs. Bickerson character." If a pilot was made, it again failed to attract interest.

The simple reason may have been that all the big money was beginning to funnel into the new, often disorganized, often cheap-looking venue of television. Phil Rapp was already gearing himself for it and the trek East to where it was all happening: New York City.

It's *Star Time*!

The hour-long variety series *Star Time* began on the DuMont network on September 5, 1950, running every Tuesday from 10 to 11 p.m. until February 27, 1951. Frances Langford, emcee Lew Parker and Benny Goodman and his band were featured in this late-night broadcast. Some references state that Don Ameche starred in this series, but according to original scripts and *Variety* reviews, Lew Parker was always the comic in charge.

The start-off show began with a marvelous variety act, including comedian Ben Blue, singer Phil Regan and dancer Kathryn Lee. Between overpowering commercials, Benny Goodman and his sextet had a brief spot to themselves, then one with Frances Langford singing her charms. Lew Parker energized a "School for Waiters" sketch from *Inside USA*. Reviewers called his bits some of the brightest of the show. With more comedy from Blue, a few classy numbers from Langford, and crooning from tenor Regan, the only thing missing in the initial show was The Bickersons, obviously since Harry Bailey, not Rapp, wrote this one.

Variety's September 13, 1950 review called *Star Time* "DuMont's most ambitious attempt at big-time TV so far, and it's a pity that the results could not have been better on the tee-off show." They criticized that the series could have used better direction and production values, though "the assembled talent was first class."

Next week's show prospered even worse and "again failed to make the grade as good video fare in its second time up. The session, despite an excellent talent lineup, was marred by poor direction and production to the point where portions of the show were both irritating and depressing." Again, the singled-out fine points of the show were Frances' singing and Lew's emceeing.

Mixed reviews were what caused Phil Rapp to get the nod to come in as writer/director. Songwriters Robert Wright and George Forest, old friends of Rapp from a few years earlier when they all collaborated on the *Spring in Brazil* musical, had produced and directed the premiere show. Naturally, they called Phil in to add some punch to the *Star Time* proceedings. One of the first things he suggested was that his brother Johnny, writer for Bob Hope, be hired to write skits and add zing. He was put on salary on October 3, 1950 at $350 a week for seven weeks, with options for many more. Reginald Gardiner and John Conte were also added to the cast.

On September 25, 1950, Rapp had signed an agreement with Stellar Enterprises to furnish The Bickersons as an independent contractor for use on *Star Time*. He would receive $1,800 per week for nine weeks, with options to extend the agreement for several 13-week periods at $2,250 per week. He would write, direct and produce the 12- to 15-minute skits. On November 17, his contract was upgraded to $3,500 a week for 13 weeks beginning on December 5th. As in all contracts he signed, Phil made sure there was a codicil assuring that the characters remained his property, not the studio's, as many writers had and have to forfeit still.

In an interview given at the time, Rapp reiterated his take that John and Blanche represented everyman and everywife. "We all know that it isn't all sugar and molasses once the honeymoon is over. Every normal couple have their family arguments and I try to depict these as truthfully as possible. When Lew Parker was suggested to me as John Bickerson, the first question I asked him was if he ever tiffed with his wife. He clinched the part with a nice, round affirmative answer!"

The basic format of an hour's worth of *Star Time* gave The Bickersons the shinning spotlight at the end, not only by closing the show, but by the fact that it had the biggest time portion allotted to it. Approximately twelve minutes was blocked off for every show. The guest spot was given over eight minutes, Frances Langford was given two numbers per episode, and Lew Parker had a comedy bit to perform for about 4.5 minutes. What with six commercials, extra songs by groups like the Delta Rhythm Boys and The Mannequins, plus John Conte's material and perhaps another guest singer, it was indeed a full hour's entertainment.

Revamped, there was immediately more interest in the variety series. One unnamed mini-review stated: "Frances Langford is really doing a job on *Star Time*. And is she happy about it! We saw her on Broadway the other day and her eyes sparkled with joy as she told us how much she enjoys her 'Mr. and Mrs. Bickerson' comedy series with Lew Parker. I understand the series is proving so popular that it may soon appear as a comic strip."

Another small article around that time claimed that Frances Langford had signed on to play in the movie version of The Bickersons, with Rapp producing and directing. Though such reports occurred infrequently in The Bickersons' multi-media run, unfortunately, a film of Rapp's legacy never, ever made it beyond the talking stage.

Star Time, however, was a hit and enough of a critical success to keep The Bickersons running, in one form or another, on television for years. Early TV audiences were hungry for variety, and variety shows, assembled in much the same way as when vaudeville was king. *Star Time*'s typical running order went as follows:

Star Time Show
Tentative Rundown
December 12, 1950

	Commercial #1 (:45)
1.	Opening (1:15)
2.	Conte Billboard (:30)
3.	Conte & Stage Manager (2:45)
4.	Frances Langford – "I Feel a Song Comin' On" (1:45)
	Intro to Comm (:10)
	Commercial #2 (1:00)
5.	Guest Room (8:45)
	Intro to Comm (:10)
	Commercial #3 (1:00)
6.	Delta Rhythm Boys (5:00)
7.	Kathryn Lee – "Dancing in the Dark" (3:40)
8.	Parker Vignette (4:30)
	Intro to Comm (:10)
	Commercial #4 (1:10)
9.	Frances Langford – "Music, Maestro, Please" (2:30)
10.	The Mannequins (3:30)
	Intro to Comm (:10)
	Commercial #5 (1:05)
	Intro (:30)

11. The Bickersons – Langford & Parker (13:00)
   Commercial #6 (1:05)
   Get Together (1:00)

TOTAL 54:20

The title song, written by Robert Wright and George Forest, opened every show, and Parker moved over to give Conte the emcee role. Much of early television relied on sight gags, but still had a radio format at heart, as this *Old Gold Show*-type sample from the December 26, 1950 episode illustrates:

(AFTER MUSICAL OPENING)

> CONTE
> Thank you, ladies and gentlemen, and welcome to *Star Time*, a new series of programs starring the lovely Frances Langford, Lew Parker, Reginald Gardiner, with Kathryn Lee – and featuring "The Bickersons." Our special guests tonight will be _____ and the internationally famous _____.

D'ARTEGA ENTERS CARRYING A SHEET OF PAPER.

> CONTE
> Tonight we have a special treat for you, and—

> D'ARTEGA (WAVING PAPER)
> I have it right here, John.

> CONTE
> Hello, D'Artega. Ladies and gentlemen, our orchestra leader, D'Artega.

(APPLAUSE)

CONTE
What have you got there, D'Artega?

D'ARTEGA (HANDING JOHN THE PAPER)
My wife doesn't think the show is funny enough, so she sent over a whole bunch of yockeritos.

CONTE
Yockeritos?

D'ARTEGA
Spanish jokes.

LEW PARKER ENTERS.

PARKER
Hello, D'Artega…Hy'a, John…What's cooking?

CONTE
Spanish yockeritos. Ever hear of 'em?

PARKER
I eat 'em all the time.

D'ARTEGA
It's nothing to eat, Lew. It's just a few jokes my wife sent up from Mexico…I'll show you… John—you read the question and I'll make the answer.

CONTE
Here goes.
(READS FROM PAPER)
Uno volte un hombre bandido de fuoco hace vestito de pantalone con rojo suspendiros…por que?

D'ARTEGA
To keep his pants up!
(TO PARKER)
Yockerito?

PARKER
Stinkerola!

D'ARTEGA
Oh. Well, that's because you didn't understand the question. Read the next joke in English and I will answer in Spanish.

CONTE (HANDING PARKER THE PAPER)

Take over, Lew.

PARKER (READING FROM PAPER)
A man had an accident with his nose that required surgery. So he had some skin grafted to his nose. Which part of his anatomy did they graft the skin from?

D'ARTEGA
(GIVES SPANISH EQUIVALENT FOR "UNDER THE SHOULDER BLADE")

CONTE
Back on your perch, D'Artega…because right now I'd like to give the downbeat for our lovely star, Frances Langford, as she sings "_____".

LANGFORD & ORCH   NUMBER
(APPLAUSE)

(AFTER CONTE – D'ARTEGA SPOT)

CONTE
Ladies and gentlemen, we invite you to sit back

and enjoy another original dance creation by our gifted and beautiful ballerina—Miss Kathryn Lee.

KATHRYN LEE: DANCE

(AFTER COMMERCIAL #2)

CONTE
And now, ladies and gentlemen, it is my pleasure to present our lovely star, Frances Langford singing "Just One of Those Things."

(LANGFORD & ORCH: "JUST ONE OF THOSE THINGS")
(APPLAUSE)

A New York promo sheet from October, 1950 stated that only something very important and close to his heart was able to extract Rapp from the mild climate of his beloved southern California. And getting The Bickersons on television was worth it.

The PR continued: "The list of stars who have wanted to play The Bickersons reads like Who's Who in Hollywood. Either part is a 'natural' for an actor because it is conceived in such human terms that the parts seem to play effortlessly. When Miss Langford read the first script, she turned to Rapp and said, 'This sounds as if you were eavesdropping in my bedroom!'"

On December 12, 1950 *The Hollywood Reporter* stated that *Star Time*'s sponsor was Grand Union Stores and was planned "for extension" to the West Coast after the first of the year. His new contract allowed Rapp to write in California for five out of his 13 weeks, choosing his own director. And again came news of "a deal in the making" for a Bickersons movie, with Rapp as writer/producer.

In Sid White's *Main Street* newspaper column he stated, "Nobody—but nobody—will ever get a Pulitzer Prize award for observing that Frances Langford can sing with the best of them—but we would like to go on record with the statement that the lovely Frances has outstanding talent as a comedienne, too. Catch her on DuMont's *Star Time* during the 'Bickerson Family' skits and see what we mean. She and her video partner, Lew Parker, do full justice to Philip Rapp's brilliantly-penned skits."

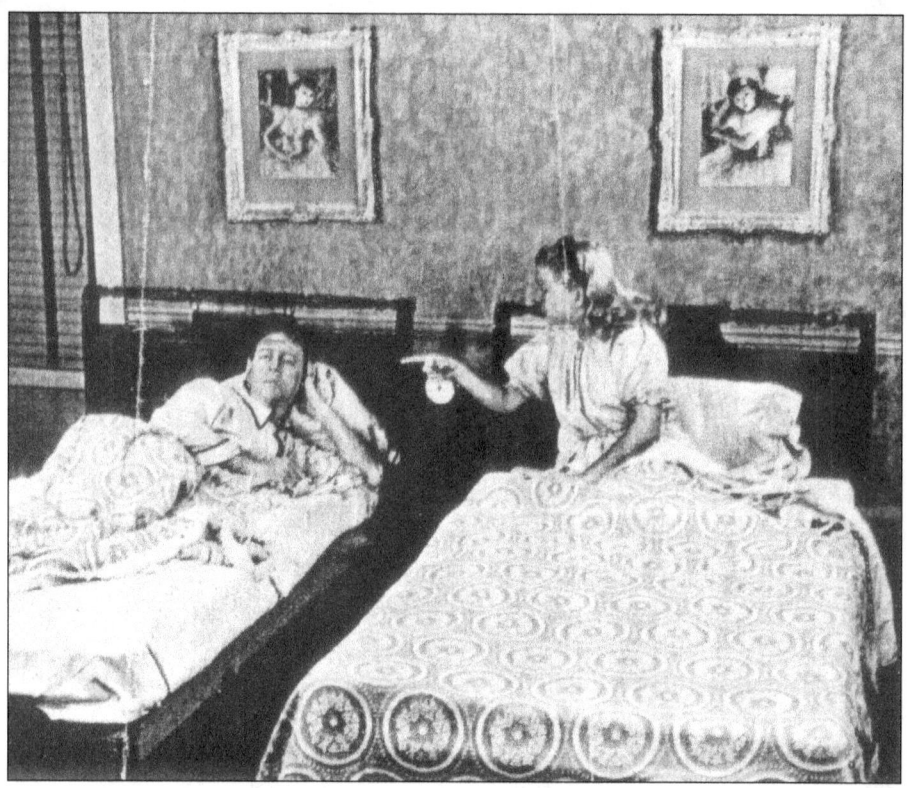

Lew and Frances on *Star Time*.

Variety reported one week that *Star Time* was the top video program in San Francisco, according to the latest Tele-Que survey, beating out *The Lone Ranger*, *Tru-Pak Movie Time* and *T-Men in Action* respectively.

John Lester's review in the *Newark Star-Ledger* was also a rave, calling it the highlight of husband and wife shows, different in that the polite, lovey-dovey conversations had no place in Rapp's heated dialogues. "Frances and Lew are so successful at this that I can say without hesitation that 'The Bickersons' is not only that high point of *Star Time* but one of the high points of all of television." All married couples saw themselves in the arguments, and Rapp's scripts were "clever, intelligent, funny, blisteringly realistic, loaded with viewer identification and a new and welcome contribution to the American TV scene."

Another untitled review was less complimentary to the surrounding components of the show, citing that the Chef Armando bit with Conte "could easily be dispensed with. It's not very funny the first time you see it, and just changing the recipe from veal cacciatore to picnic basket lunches doesn't make it any funnier." It called The Bickersons far superior to the rest of the package and urged someone just to extract those 15 minutes out. It praised Lew Parker, claiming that he "gets more out of the character and situations than Don Ameche got out of them on AM." Frances was called perfect as the nagging wife, of course, though they wished that when she sang her numbers, she would "wear gowns not quite so tight." It complimented Phil Rapp's writings as being largely responsible "for the bit's wow qualities."

Al Morton, in his *TV Roundup* column, didn't mind Frances' evening gowns and also glorified The Bickersons as the bright light of the musical comedy hour. "Numerous other comedy skits are interspersed throughout the show but emerge hopelessly overshadowed by the saga of the battling Bickersons." But he conceded that John Conte, Reginald Gardiner and Kathryn Lee "round out a cast that will give you a consistently good hour of entertainment."

The latest Ross Poll cited *Star Time* as one of two "most steadily improved" attractions for TV, which perked up the show's sponsors: Grand Union Market, Snow Crop, McCormick Extracts, Roylies Doilies, and Chef Boyardee.

One Senior Productions budget showed the two highest paid performers of the show, of course, were Frances Langford (gross $1,125) and Lew Parker ($750). The three others in the cast, Peter Leeds, Benny Rubin and Doris Singleton, received $80 a piece, while the total cost for writers was $500. The one day's show total, with many music bills to pay, came in at $5,045.

The Bickersons' comedy was largely not rewritten for television. Sight gags were added, but as the below December 26, 1950 episode again shows, it was nearly word-for-word radio comedy, visualized:

(LANGFORD & ORCH: "JUST ONE OF THOSE THINGS")
(APPLAUSE)
                    GUEST ROOM
(DISCOVERED: John Conte at the bar, using the phone)

                CONTE (on phone)
What's that?...you say Mr. Gardiner left for the theatre hours ago?...Well, he hasn't shown up here yet...All right—I'll have him call you when he gets in.

(As he hangs up Lew Parker enters carrying a large can of cleaning fluid and a rag)

          PARKER
Hy'a, John. Would you let me have a glass, please?

          CONTE
Sure, Lew.
(Hands him glass)
What's that stuff you got there?

          PARKER
It's a cleaning mixture I got from Johnny the stagehand.
(Pours some into glass)
I brushed up against some fresh scenery and got some paint on my coat. Got any water there? I have to dilute it, this stuff is powerful.

          CONTE (handing him pitcher of water)
Sure…Here.

(Reggie Gardiner rushes in. He is in a high state of excitement)

          GARDINER
Quickly, Charlie! Fix me a triple brandy and spray some soda on the outside of the glass. Hurry!

          CONTE
Reggie Gardiner!

(APPLAUSE)

          GARDINER (to Parker who is stirring the concoction)

Don't hog that drink, Charlie—I tell you this is a matter of life and death.

>PARKER (as he struggles to retain possession of the glass)
>Now wait a minute, Reggie —

>GARDINER
>Let go of it!
(He pries the glass loose and downs its contents)
>There!...Charlie, I must say that you have the tenacity of a bulldog without it's compensating beauty.

>PARKER
>Well, I don't know about me—but you just drank some paint remover!

>GARDINER
>Paint remover!

>PARKER
>I'll send over a stomach pump for a chaser. So long, boys.

(He exits)

>CONTE
>He tried to warn you, Reggie.

>GARDINER
>Well, I was going to have an interior decorator re-do my interior, anyway. Fix me a brandy chaser, Jockey, I've just had the most horrible experience.

>CONTE
>You're shaking like a leaf!

GARDINER
My boy, you're looking at a man who's lived through the greatest catastrophe since the Boxer Rebellion!

CONTE
I wondered why you were late. What happened?

GARDINER
I was driving to the theatre tonight at a moderate rate of speed, accompanied by an old friend—a charming thing whose acquaintance I made at a bus stop.

CONTE
Bus stop.

GARDINER
While waiting for the lights to change. My companion was a demure young lady—very straight-laced in a loose sort of a way. We were discussing her singing career, when the accident happened.

CONTE
What accident?

GARDINER
As I said before, we were driving slowly down Broadway on my way to the theatre, when I decided to take a short cut through Peapack, New Jersey.

CONTE
Short cut?

GARDINER
The scenic route.

CONTE
Broadway to the theatre and you go through New Jersey? Sounds like you were just wasting time.

GARDINER
Unfortunately I was. But I didn't find that out till I saw her wedding ring. It was then I began to realize my clutch was slipping. On the car, of course.

CONTE
Of course.

GARDINER
Of course. At any rate, I headed back to town on the main road, driving very carefully with both hands on the girl—wheel—when suddenly, I saw careening towards me a heavy car, obviously out of control. By an amazing piece of quick thinking I managed to meet him head on!

CONTE
That's using your head. Where is the girl now?

GARDINER
She's in my dressing room recovering from shock—and I'd like to enlist your aid in bringing her the proper medication.

CONTE
All right. I'll phone the drugstore and order—

GARDINER
There's no time for that—just send up two shakers of martinis and a portable radio.

CONTE
Fine shock treatment! That girl should be kept warm and have nothing but quiet and rest.

GARDINER
Well, the martinis will warm her up, the radio will keep her quiet, and I'll do the rest. I've already sent for a nurse and she'll be—

(Frances Langford enters)

LANG
Evening, gentlemen. Am I late?

GARDINER
Oh, hello, my dear! You're just in time! You must be the nurse I ordered from Bellevue. Turn around and let me have a better view, Belle.

LANG
I beg your pardon?

GARDINER
You may get into your uniform, dear. I'll pay you double for overtime, over for double-time and time and a half for time. What time is it?

LANG
Half past ten.

GARDINER
Well, that's enough work for today. Shall we dine together?

CONTE
Reggie!

GARDINER
What?

CONTE
How is it possible that you can walk in here four

weeks in a row and don't recognize Frances Langford's face?

GARDINER
Very simple—I haven't reached there yet.

CONTE
Reggie! For the last time—this is Francis Langford our singing star.

GARDINER
Oh, Frances Startime. Of course! May I say that I've enjoyed your singing immensely for many years.

LANG
Thank you.

GARDINER
Of course, I do think you should make better use of your diaphragm—sort of emphasize your cadenzas—lift your octaves a little above your solfeggio and shave down your middle register. What time can you come for a lesson, my little bullfinch?

LANG
I'm afraid I—

GARDINER
Inside of six months I'll have the Diamond Horseshoe at your feet—you'll be presented at all the famous halls—Exposition Hall in San Francisco, Whitehall in London and Carnegie Hall, New York.

LANG
What about Jon Hall in Hollywood?

GARDINER
Oh, is that your ambition?

LANG
No, it's my husband.

GARDINER
Err—husband.

LANG
Goodnight, Mr. Gardiner.

(She exits)

GARDINER
Lovely child. Pity she's married. We could have made such beautiful music together.

CONTE
Music!

GARDINER
She's such a gifted soprano and I'm so bass. Well, I imagine I'd better get back to my young friend. Is anything going to happen here right now?

CONTE
Not much. D'Artega's going to conduct "Dance of the Hours" from Ponchielli's "La Giaconda," that's all.

GARDINER
You can't possibly mean that, Conte!

CONTE
Don't you like that piece of music?

GARDINER
It's beautiful! But the thought of that heavy-hand-

ed D'Artega swinging a baton to such a delicate, lacy, and difficult composition leaves me aghast.

D'ARTEGA
Excuse me, Mr. Gardiner.

GARDINER
Yes?

D'ARTEGA
You don't like the way I conduct?

GARDINER
Well, I didn't mean—

CONTE
You're in it now, Reggie. Why don't *you* conduct it?

GARDINER
A splendid idea, Johnson. Let me have that baton, Teagarden.

D'ARTEGA
D'Artega.

GARDINER
Yes.
(He takes the baton)
You just run back there to your little cave and play with your glockenspiel…
(Lifts baton)
Ready, gentlemen. Glissando, con molto esspressione!

DANCE OF THE HOURS
(AFTER COMMERCIAL #3)

CONTE
Get set to enjoy a most novel and original singing group transplanted from California where they created a sensation—here they are "The Whippoorwills."

WHIPPOORWILLS: 2 NUMBERS

(APPLAUSE)

PARKER COOKING VIGNETTE

SCENE: CORNER OF A KITCHEN...SHOWING TELEVISION SET...KITCHEN TABLE AND STOVE.

DISCOVERED: LEW PARKER ENTERS AND PLACES AN ARMFUL OF GROCERIES ON THE TABLE. THEN HE GOES TO THE TELEVISION SET AND TURNS IT ON)

PARKER
Tonight I'm gonna learn how to make a meal out of kitchen scraps.

(JOHN CONTE'S FACE APPEARS ON TELEVISION SCREEN)

CONTE
Good evening, all you amateur cooks. This is Chef Armando, the Weasel of the Oven and tonight I'ma gonna teach you how to make the best use of you holiday leftover food. First...go to the place where you store you leftovers and put 'em on the table.

(PARKER DEPRESSES LEVER ON SMALL GARBAGE CAN NEAR LEG OF TABLE, TAKES FROM IT A DRESSED CHICKEN, HALF A SALAMI, AND THE RINDS OF TWO GRAPEFRUIT HALFS. HE PLACES THESE ON TABLE)

CONTE

All right...now out of you left-overs we gonna make Neapolitan ghoulash ala Armando... Ready?...Okay...We start with the wine sauce... You got any left-over chianti?...Fine...Pour a dash into you pot.

(PARKER DOES SO)

Now add to this two cups of left-over white wine...half a lemon...a jigger of brandy...a splash of scotch...and put in some rye.

(PARKER POURS IN THE ABOVE INGREDIENTS RAPIDLY...FINISHING BY DROPPING IN HALF A LOAF OF RYE BREAD)

Fine...now mix this together and see if it's sweet enough.

(PARKER MIXES IT, THEN TAKES DIPPERFUL, DRINKS IT, SMACKS HIS LIPS SPECULATIVELY AND POURS IN HALF A BOTTLE OF WHISKEY AND A PINCH OF SUGAR...HE STIRS IT WITH THE BREAD)

Good...now put the pot on the stove and let it simmer, while we work on our ghoulash.

(HE PUTS POT ON STOVE...TAKING ANOTHER DRINK AS HE DOES SO)

Right offa the bat you take'a you left-over salami and grind him up in you meat grinder.

(PARKER PUSHES SALAMI DOWN INTO TOP OF MEAT GRINDER AND FORCES OUT SMALL COCKTAIL SAUSAGES CONCEALED IN GRINDING APERTURE. HE THROWS THEM IN MIXING BOWL)

CONTE
Now add to this some parsely, celery and two eggs.

(PARKER PUTS PARSLEY, CELERY AND TWO WHOLE EGGS INTO TOP OF MEAT GRINDER AND STARTS TO GRIND... AS HE GRINDS HE SINGS A LITTLE OF "O, SOLE MIO")

Hey, wait a minoots!...it's a time to checka you wine sauce...go ahead, check it!

(PARKER DIPS DIPPER INTO WINE SAUCE ON STOVE AND TAKES A HEALTHY SWALLOW)

Is it strong enough?

(PARKER FILLS DIPPER, BRINGS IT TO CONTE, WHO TAKES A DRINK)

Add some raisins and a dash of brandy.

(PARKER DROPS IN ONE RAISIN AND POURS IN A BIG SHOT OF BRANDY...THEN HE SAMPLES IT AGAIN... BRINGS CONTE A DRINK)

Joost'a right...okay...now take'a some left-over stewed meat...but make'a sure it'sa stewed.

(PARKER DUNKS ALREADY-COOKED STEAK INTO WINE SAUCE COUPLE OF TIMES...HE LICKS IT AND SMILES)

Now dice you stewed meat carefully...make sure you dice him even.

(PARKER CUTS A COUPLE OF CUBES FROM STEAK)

Next you pick up these diced cubes and roll 'em in flour.

(PARKER SPRINKLES FLOUR ON BOARD, PICKS UP THE TWO CUBES OF MEAT AND IN CRAPSHOOTER FASHION HE ROLLS THEM OUT ONTO BOARD AND SNAPS HIS FINGERS...THEN HE THROWS THEM IN BOWL)

Tak'a some of you left-over mashed potatoes, make them into balls and throw 'em in too.

(PARKER PUTS HIS HAND INTO POT OF MASHED POTATOES, MAKES A BIG SNOWBALL, WINDS UP AND TOSSES IT IN POT)

Then you add to this mess the juice of two tomatoes.

(PARKER SQUEEZES TWO TOMATOES IN HIS HANDS AND DROPS THEM IN BOWL)

Nice'a work...we gonna have everything in'a good taste.

(PARKER HOLDS HIS HAND UP TO STOP CHEF... FILLS DIPPER WITH WINE SAUCE, DRINKS IT...DIPS IT IN AGAIN, BRINGS IT TO JOHN, WHO TAKES ANOTHER DRINK)

CONTE (Slightly tipsy)
Now you take'a some cubumber and cacon... scooz...I mean bakecumber and cewkon... cuccumber and bacon...that'sa right...wrap them up together sealing the cuccumber inside.

(PARKER TAKES WHOLE CUCUMBER AND HALF A POUND OF FLAT SLICED BACON...HE PLACES CUCUMBER ON BACON...FOLDS OVER THE BACON... THEN PICKS UP STAPLER AND STAPLES ACROSS TWO

FOLDED ENDS OF BACON. HE HOLDS IT UP THEN DROPS IT IN BOWL)

> Next we add you left-over chicken to the bowl…first make sure the chicken is cleaned and dressed.

(PARKER PLACES DIAPER TRIANGLE ON TABLE…PUTS CHICKEN ON IT…THEN HE PICKS UP LEGS OF CHICKEN …POWDERS HIM WITH TALCUM…FOLDS DIAPER OVER CHICKEN AND HOLDS IT IN PLACE WITH SAFETY PIN… THEN HE PICKS IT UP, PLACES IT ON HIS SHOULDER, PATS IT TO BURP IT, THEN DROPS IT INTO BOWL)

> That's a beautiful…now i think we got everything loaded, so—

(PARKER HOLDS UP HIS HAND TO STOP CHEF, DIPS DIPPER INTO WINE SAUCE, TAKES A BIG DRINK… THEN HE STAGGERS OVER TO JOHN…GIVES HIM A DRINK…POURING SOME ON HIM IN THE PROCESS)

> Next you grab hold of you olive oil…and pour oil on you chicken…pour it on you stewed meat…pour it on everything.

(PARKER WIELDS OLIVE IN A FANCY MANNER OVER THE BOWL…PRETENDS TO POUR A LITTLE ON HIS HANDS AND DABS HIMSELF BEHIND THE EARS WITH IT)

> Now…is everything well oiled?

(PARKER HOLDS UP HIS HAND TO CHEF AGAIN…GOES TO WINE SAUCE…TAKES A BIG SWIG…BRINGS BOTTLE OVER TO JOHN…WHO DRINKS FROM BOTTLE)

> CONTE (He's really woozy now)
> Hold everything…I think I'm a gettin' a little blurred.

(PARKER TUNES IN KNOB ON TELEVISION SET. THIS CAUSES CONTE TO STRAIGHTEN UP FROM STOOPED POSITION, HE STOPS GRIMACING AND SMILES... THEN HE HOLDS HIS HEAD)

> Okay...now you (hiccups) scooza, please...now you put'a you stove in the bowl and squeeze'a the juice of a two dishpans...oooh...I'm think my head is killing me...you better figger out the next move.

(PARKER TAKES TWO GLASSES FULL OF WATER... DROPS IN FIVE ALKA SELTZERS IN EACH GLASS... HANDS ONE TO JOHN AS IT FIZZES...AND WE DISSOLVE AS THEY OFFER A TOAST)

(AFTER COMMERCIAL # 4)

> CONTE
> Here's Frances Langford, ladies and gentlemen, to sing for you Hoagy Carmichael's perennial favorite—"Stardust."

LANG: "STARDUST"

(APPLAUSE)

> CONTE
> Thank you, Frances—that was beautiful...A change of pace right now as we present those madcap, musical merrymakers—the celebrated "Irving Fields Trio."

IRVING FIELDS TRIO: TWO NUMBERS

(APPLAUSE)

<u>THE BICKERSONS</u>

                    CONTE
And now, ladies and gentlemen, here are Frances
Langford and Lew Parker as John and Blanche
Bickerson in "The Honeymoon is over."

THEME: (SOFT AND PLAINTIVE)

                    CONTE
Blanche Bickerson has finally realized her fondest
dream, a new and larger home. It is past midnight and the moving man is carting the last of
the Bickerson's belongings into the spacious six-
room apartment as the watchful Blanche super-
vises the unloading.

FADE IN new Bickerson apartment.

(Blanche in her hat and coat, stands in the middle of the room. All about the place are signs of having just moved in. A barrel stands near the dresser—two suitcases are by one wall—a carton is piled on top of the suitcases. The moving man, in overalls is bringing another barrel into the room)

                    MAN
Where do you want this, lady?

                    BLANCHE
Leave it right there for the time being.

                    MAN
Yes, ma'am.

                    BLANCHE
I never realized we had so much stuff. Isn't it
funny how people hang onto all kinds of junk?

                    MAN
Yes, ma'am.

BLANCHE
I guess all married people are like that. Are you married?

MAN
No, ma'am. I look this way from carryin' heavy furniture.

BLANCHE
Oh. Are there any other large pieces on the trunk?

MAN
Yes, ma'am. I gotta bring the stove up. They shoulda give me another man to help me.

BLANCHE
I thought my husband was helping you. Where is he?

MAN
I ain't seen him since I took his bed apart at your old place. It wasn't easy with him still in it.

BLANCHE
Well, my husband works very hard and he needs his sleep…

MAN
I didn't wake him up. I propped him against the wall with a bedslat. He was gone when I come up for the barrels.

BLANCHE
Well, he's probably down at the truck. You go get the stove.

(Man exits carrying dolly. Blanche picks up carton, starts toward kitchen and stops suddenly as she reaches the barrel. From inside the barrel comes the sound of John's snoring. Blanche stares, then pulls the sheet off)

JOHN (snores and whines)

BLANCHE
John Bickerson! What are you doing in that barrel?

JOHN (a protesting whine)
Mmmmmmm.

BLANCHE
Get out, get out, get out!

JOHN (putting his head out.
He wears a hat)
Get out, Blanche. Wassamatter? Why don't you let me sleep? Whaddya want, Blanche?

BLANCHE
Get out of that barrel! I'll bet you've broken all my dishes!

JOHN
Only one.
  (he hands her a chafing dish)
Here.

BLANCHE
What did you do that for? You broke the handle off my chafing dish.

JOHN
Well, it was chafing me. Goodnight.
(He ducks in the barrel)

BLANCHE
Don't you curl up in there again!

JOHN
Please, Blanche, I can't keep my eyes open. Go to sleep.

BLANCHE
I can't go to sleep. My bed is piled high with my clothes.

JOHN
Crawl in the other barrel.

BLANCHE
You're insane. I'd smother to death.

JOHN
Stick your nose through the bunghole. Put out the lights.

BLANCHE
(pulling him out of the barrel)
You get out of that thing! And put away my clothes.

(He gets out of the barrel, revealing himself in pajamas and bare feet)

JOHN
Put out the lights.

BLANCHE
I will not! You just put my clothes away neatly while I straighten out the bathroom.

(She goes to the bathroom. He takes all her clothes off the bed dumps them into the barrel with the dishes. Then he gets into his bed. No sooner does he get settled when door buzzer rings)

BLANCHE'S VOICE (O.S.)
John!

JOHN
Mmm?

BLANCHE'S VOICE
Get the door.

JOHN
I got the door. I packed it away with the windows.

BLANCHE'S VOICE
It's the moving man with the stove! Go let him in!

(He gets out of bed, starts looking for his slipper)

JOHN
Where's my slipper?

BLANCHE'S VOICE
You packed it away yourself.

JOHN
Oh, yeah.

(He goes to the suitcases, opens a small overnight bag, throws all the stuff out, finds his slipper which is attached to a three-foot chain. The chain is attached to the inside of the bag. He tries to detach the slipper. It won't come away)

SOUND: DOOR BUZZER

JOHN (still struggling with the slipper)
Wait a minute! I'm coming!

BLANCHE'S VOICE
What's taking you so long?

JOHN
I got my slipper chained to the bag and I can't unhook it.

BLANCHE (poking her head thru door)
What did you do that for?

JOHN
It's the only one I've got and I didn't want to take a chance on loosing it.

BLANCHE
Oh, stop fooling with it, and let the man in.

(She goes back into the bathroom. He puts the slipper on, goes to the door dragging the bag with the chain. He opens the door and let's the moving man in. The moving man has the stove on a dolly, he wheels it straight across to the kitchen. He returns carrying a dolly)

MAN
That's the last of it.

JOHN
You got everything?

MAN (reading from list)
Yes, sir. Two beds, one bureau, three barrels, eleven suitcases, two trunks, four cartons, one crate, one table and four chairs, radio stove and refrigerator, nine cases of bourbon and one icebag.

JOHN
How much do I owe you?

MAN
Nineteen dollars and seventy-five cents.

JOHN (reaching into his grouchbag)
All I got is a twenty dollar bill. Have you got change?

MAN
No. But I'll carry the stove down and bring it up again if you want me to work out the extra quarter.

JOHN
Wise guy. Keep the quarter.

MAN
Thanks. Here's your receipt.
    (hands him receipt as he goes)
Two bits for breakin' my back—I shoulda been a bookmaker.

(He exits. John walks to bed, takes off his slipper, and gets in. Blanche enters in her nightgown, gets in bed)

BLANCHE
I still don't think we ought to go to sleep without putting the apartment in order. Let's take inventory, John.

JOHN
Why do you have to do it now? Can't I have a few minutes rest?

BLANCHE
You'll have plenty of time to rest when you go to work. Take that pad and call off the things as I check them.

JOHN (reaching for pad on night table)
A bunch of mustard greens, a pound of chicken gizzards, half a pint of cottonseed oil—

BLANCHE
That's my shopping list.

JOHN
Shopping list?

BLANCHE
Yes, I'm going to bake a cake.

JOHN
A cake! With chicken gizzards?

BLANCHE
Don't be silly. That's for the cat. Take the other—John! The cat!

JOHN
What about him?

BLANCHE
Where is he? He's lost and it's all your fault! I begged you to take care of him and see that he got here safely!

JOHN
He'll get here. They'll deliver him in the morning.

BLANCHE
How do you know?

JOHN
I put him in a sack and dropped him in the mailbox.

BLANCHE
John! You didn't!

JOHN
Oh, Blanche, I didn't put him in any mailbox.

BLANCHE
Well, don't scare me like that. You'd better go out and look for him, John.

JOHN
Blanche, I guarantee you that cat'll be here in the morning.

BLANCHE
What makes you so sure?

JOHN
Because I tied a label around his neck with our new address on it.

BLANCHE
What good is that? He can't read.

JOHN
I know he can't read! But people can read and somebody's bound to pick him up and deliver him—heaven forbid.

BLANCHE
You hate that cat, don't you?

JOHN
I don't hate him at all.

BLANCHE
You do, too!

JOHN
I do not!! I love the cat, I love the canary and I love you! I don't know which one of you I love most!

BLANCHE
You don't love any of us.

JOHN
Yes I do.

BLANCHE
Well, if the house ever caught fire which would you save first? The cat, the canary, or me?

JOHN
Me. Blanche, you know I have to get up so early in the morning—why don't you let me sleep?

BLANCHE
I don't see how you can sleep, anyway. Haven't you got any romance in your soul?

JOHN
Blanche, it's almost two o'clock in the morning.

BLANCHE
I don't care. For the first time since we got married we have a real home and you didn't even carry me across the threshold.

JOHN
Carry you across the threshold! That's for newlyweds.

BLANCHE
What of it? We've only been married eight years.

JOHN
Well, I can't carry a grudge that long. Go to sleep.

BLANCHE
I don't understand you, I swear I don't. Aren't you even going to kiss me goodnight?

JOHN
Again? I kissed you goodnight last night, didn't I?

BLANCHE
Is it such a terrible chore to kiss your wife goodnight everynight? Am I so distasteful to you? Does it hurt you to kiss me?

JOHN
Don't feel a thing.

BLANCHE
That's because you have no feelings at all! Here we are our first night in a brand new apartment—just like a second honeymoon and you're acting like an old worn-out married man.

JOHN
I'm not acting. Put out the lights.

BLANCHE
I'd like to hear you say that to Gloria Gooseby.

JOHN
Now don't start with Gloria Gooseby.

BLANCHE
Believe me, if Gloria Gooseby had to ask for a kiss you wouldn't say "put out the lights."

JOHN
She never has to ask for it and I always put out the lights! I mean, I hate Gloria Gooseby and I'd like to spend one night of my life without her!

BLANCHE
Oh, is that where you've been spending your nights?

JOHN
Now listen, Blanche—you promised when we got this new apartment you wouldn't beef anymore. What's the matter with you? Why are you carrying on like this?

BLANCHE
Well, I've got something to tell you.

JOHN
Well, tell me.

BLANCHE

If you give me a kiss I'll tell you.

JOHN
Tell me now and I'll kiss you later.

BLANCHE
You might not feel like kissing me later.

JOHN
I don't feel like kissing you now. Not after the way you upset me. What have you done?

BLANCHE
Well, after all, we're starting a new married life, aren't we?

JOHN
Mmm.

BLANCHE
So to insure our future happiness I've arranged for us to have another wedding. Clara and Barney thought up the idea.

JOHN
Another wedding!

BLANCHE
It's going to be a formal wedding and we're having the ceremony and wedding supper at Lum Fong's.

JOHN
Lum Fong's!

BLANCHE
Barney's a waiter there and we're going to split the tips!

JOHN
I'll split his head! Listen Blanche, you call that thing off.

BLANCHE
I can't. I've already sent out the invitations.

JOHN
I don't care! I'm not going to have any formal wedding just to feed your hungry friends and their squalling brats.

BLANCHE
There aren't going to be any brats there at all.

JOHN
They'll bring their kids, I tell you!

BLANCHE
No, they won't. It says plainly on the invitation "Mr. and Mrs. John Bickerson will be married on February 12th. No children expected."

JOHN
The wedding's off, Blanche. February 12th is a Tuesday and I've gotta work.

BLANCHE
No, you don't. February 12th happens to be Lincoln's birthday. That's why I chose it to get married.

JOHN
A fine present for the man who freed the slaves. Put out the lights.

BLANCHE
Not just yet. If we're going to have a wedding then you're going to have to ask for my hand. Go on, John—propose to me.

JOHN
I'll propose to you in the morning.

BLANCHE
You say it, but you won't do it. Do it now.

JOHN
What!

BLANCHE
Go on, get up and propose to me!

JOHN
Oh, nobody would believe this.

BLANCHE
I'm waiting, John.

JOHN
Okay. Will you marry me?

BLANCHE
That's not the way to say it. I want you to get out of bed and say it.

(He gets out of bed, puts his slipper on)

JOHN
This must all be a bad dream.

BLANCHE
Come around here, take my hand, get down on your knee and be romantic and poetic.

(He kneels down by her bed and takes her hand.)

JOHN
Darling woman of my derams, I love you more than pork and beans—

BLANCHE
Stop that! Propose to me properly.

JOHN
Dear Sweet Blanche, my love for you knows no bounds. I know I'm not worthy of you—but will you consent to be my wife?

BLANCHE
No.

JOHN
No!?

BLANCHE
You don't sound sincere enough. I want you to say it with real emotion.

JOHN
You're out of your mind. I'm not gonna propose to you and what's more, I'm not getting married again.

(He goes back to bed, puts the slipper in the satchel and puts the satchel under his pillow. He gets in bed and pulls up the covers)

BLANCHE
I knew it. You're sorry you married me the first time.

JOHN
I never said that.

BLANCHE
You don't have to say it—I feel it. You hate me.

JOHN
Oh, Blanche, I don't hate you.

BLANCHE
You do, you do, you do!

JOHN
I tell you I don't!

BLANCHE
Do you love me?

JOHN
Yes.

BLANCHE
Then why don't you ever say it?

JOHN
I say it all the time. I've taken ads in the paper saying I love you—I've got "I love you Blanche" embroidered on my shorts—I even tried to write it in blood but you wouldn't let me, would you?

BLANCHE
No.

JOHN
Why wouldn't you let me write it in blood, Blanche?

BLANCHE
Because the needle was hurting my finger.

JOHN
Well, I would have done it myself if I wasn't so anemic. Please put out the lights and let me get some sleep, Blanche.

BLANCHE
I never expected the first night in our new apartment would be like this. I've been looking forward to this day for years.

JOHN
Mmm.

BLANCHE
Don't you like the place, John?

JOHN
I don't know, I haven't seen it.

BLANCHE
I know we can be happy here. There are six rooms, it has a wonderful kitchen, and the bathroom is out of this world.

JOHN
That's what I was afraid of. You still haven't told me what the rent is.

BLANCHE
Thirty dollars a month.

JOHN
Thirty dollars a month! We were paying fifty for that one-room goat's nest we lived in. How did you do it, Blanche?

BLANCHE
Oh, I just used my head. I'm not as stupid as you think I am, you know.

JOHN
I'm sure you're not. Did you set the alarm clock?

BLANCHE
Yes, I set it.

JOHN
For six-thirty?

BLANCHE
Four-thirty.

JOHN
Four-thirty? Who gets up at four-thirty?

BLANCHE
You do. You have to bank the furnace.

JOHN
What are you talking about? This is an apartment house, the janitor banks the furnace.

BLANCHE
You're the janitor.

JOHN
What?!

BLANCHE
How do you think I got the apartment so cheap?

JOHN
I won't do it! I won't do it, I tell you! I work seventeen hours a day at the office—I'm not going to come home and scrub the floors—and be a janitor! We're getting out of here, do you hear me? Tonight!

BLANCHE
Wait a minute, John—don't be hasty. Just listen to reason.

JOHN
I'm deaf.

> BLANCHE
> I must have this apartment, it's got an extra bedroom.

> JOHN
> We don't need an extra bedroom. One bedroom is enough for the two of us.

> BLANCHE
> John, you don't understand. It isn't always going to be the two of us. I only found out today that in a few months we're going to have another mouth to feed.

> JOHN
> Blanche! You mean…

> BLANCHE
> Yes. My mother is coming to live with us!

> JOHN
> Goodnight, Blanche.

> BLANCHE
> Goodnight, John.

CURTAIN

For whatever reason, *Star Time* sang its last on February 27, 1951. The high-profile series and eager Bickersons reviews attracted yet another sponsor who had found so much mileage in radio: Philip Morris. Phil Rapp was happy to take his married couple back to their original medium, though Don Ameche had other live television commitments and could not rejoin the series which was finally getting its own half-hour time slot. Lew Parker again proved himself a more than able vacuum cleaner salesman.

The 1951 Series

The *Bickersons* radio show with Frances and Lew began on June 5, 1951 over WCBS (originating from Station WNX-CBS, California), as a summer replacement for *Truth or Consequences*. When John and Blanche came back to radio, a fan and *New York Herald Tribune* columnist again gave a significant rave for their contrast to the usual type of family entertainment. Though he couldn't recall "a single likable character" in the show's short career, he thought the reason the series worked so well was because "you can feel both sorry for and superior to The Bickersons, which is a very pleasant emotional mixture." He likened Rapp's attitude to women, children and people in general to Al Capp, the *Li'l Abner* cartoonist: all humor is sadistic.

Frances Langford had begun receiving top billing when Lew Parker took over John's role. In the new series, Lew would have a few words before the show began, then introduced "Ms. Purple Heart Girl," Frances, who then sang a song. The notable extra about the 1951 show was that new material had to be written for each episode in order to flesh it out to a half-hour or to link two previous small skits together into a whole story. At last, there were new jokes and new situations for the accursed couple.

Weekly Variety's June 13, 1951 review of the new Langford-Parker series thought there was "real bite" in the fighting dialogue, but wished there had been more situational humor combined with it to keep the series from becoming too repetitive and stifled in one setting. It liked Langford's "Blue Skies" but thought it slowed the opening and wished numbers could somehow be integrated into the story line. It praised the fine casting, though thought Lurene Tuttle, Lou Lubin, Benny Rubin and John Brown were underused (as they were). Also, the Philip Morris commercials were starting to lose their impact due to constant repetition.

Seventeen days later, Rapp signed an agreement with Wald-Krasna Productions to write *The U.S.O. Story*, an RKO picture, at the salary of $2,500 per week. Again, a clause was included giving Rapp time off for his Bickersons show.

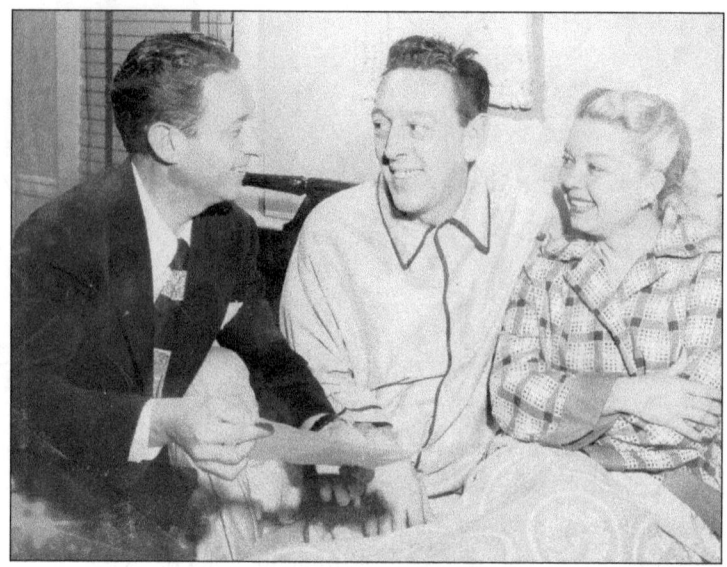

Phil, Lew and Frances.

In the anniversary party episode, Barney can't come to the fete since he's going to a masquerade party in which everyone has to dress as a bum, so naturally he wants to borrow some of John's clothes. John, meanwhile, is busy *not* selling vacuum cleaners door-to-door. He goes back to the company and admits to a co-worker that he got sentimental and bought Blanche a diamond ring for their anniversary: nothing down and $10 a week for life. He's three weeks behind on the first payment. He tries to pawn his sample vacuum but is turned in by the suspicious shopkeeper as the local and active Cat Burglar.

The middle commercial takes a non-Philip Morris smoker and gives him a ciggie taste test in a supposedly unscripted testimonial. "No payment is made for any statement in the interview." Of course, all volunteers always gave the same result: the Philip Morris smoke was *milder* than their current brand. On one particular Bickersons episode, the opening announcer loftily intoned that "in the previous year, Philip Morris has gained more smokers than all other leading brands combined. No other cigarette can make that statement." (Based on "official releases by the United States government.")

The pitches were carefully sculpted, and *very* consequential to the sponsor. As stated in these December 13, 1951 notes from "Philip Morris" to Rapp, it's clear that every word, every emphasis was vigilantly haggled over:

"We have been using the following line as a kind of 'wrap-up' for our commercials: 'You'll be *glad* you smoked Philip Morris today!'

"This is a pretty important line because it implies a hell of a lot more than we can actually state in copy. I think you should use this line whenever possible. It can be *mildly* gagged. It might, perhaps, make a 'running line' or a double entendre snapper as the last line of a dialogue sequence.

"One angle we have been playing up recently—and I expect we will stay with it for a while—is the fact that you enjoy Philip Morris *all day long*, from your very first cigarette in the morning to your last cigarette at night. The point is that because Philip Morris is less irritating, the smoker avoids the dry throat and the stale taste that normally results from smoking other cigarettes all day long. The implication, which we sometimes state, is that Philip Morris leaves your throat clear and clean, your taste unblunted. We speak of the 'unique pleasure' and the 'exclusive protection' which the smoker enjoys in Philip Morris."

Other angles pointed out were that smoking a Philip Morris "breaks the ice" when in social situations, and that the tension of these trying, modern times would be *so much* alleviated by lighting up a smooth, relaxing smoke. All jokes about chain smokers and cigarettes being a narcotic were strictly verboten.

The commercials may have been heavy-handed and repetitive, but like everyone else at the time, Philip Morris gave up radio in favor of television. An August 21, 1951 telegram from Biow Co., acting as agent for Philip Morris, stated that the show had been cancelled. After a mere 13 episodes of what might have been a very funny and long run, The Bickersons also, and with finality, deserted the airwaves for the new medium.

By the end of the summer of 1951, The Bickersons tried to repeat their television success with six half-hour shows starring Lew Parker and the very beautiful Virginia Grey. *It's the Bickersons* was recorded in front of a live audience and therefore did not have the cheap, reading-the-cue-cards look that many contemporary live-broadcast shows (at least, of the variety-type that The Bickersons found themselves on as guests) had. The series is now available on two DVDs, with extras.

Phil didn't care for cue cards. He made his stars memorize every script to enhance the timing so necessary to his rapid-fire dialogue. He also hated canned laughter, sometimes so necessary to the studio mentality. "I knew the networks would insist on a laugh track, and this would spoil The Bickersons. When they're wound up, they talk right over the laughs of the live audiences in the studio. A laugh track would ruin the timing."

Each show did not begin with its usual theme tune, but a more swirling, romantic piece of music as two little lovebirds (parakeets) chirped

away, finally separating to let the title credits show through.

The TV cast included: Clara (Lois Austin), Barney (Sam Lee), Dr. Hersey (William Pullen), Marvin (Arthur Lovejoy), Detective (Al Shaw), and Jailer (Robert Carraher). Production crew: Assistant Director (Robert Agnew), Cameraman (Frederick Gately), Art Director (Frank Sylos), Film Editor (Stanley Rabjohn). After the intrusive end credits, the birds huddled back together.

Rapp reused all of the material he'd written for the previous '51 radio series, as well as recycled sight gags from previous TV reincarnations (such as Nature Boy jumping out of the huge refrigerator). New material may have helped the series sell, but he did adapt the skits a bit when The Bickersons played guest spots on the many live shows that made them hugely sought after. On November 19, 1951, Phil licensed the couple (Lew and Virginia) and "suitable script" to Ed Wynn for $3,000 to use on his *All-Star Review* on December 8, 1951. Though Rapp wrote, produced and directed the entire show, *The Hollywood Reporter* thought The Bickersons was the highlight. "No one can touch [Rapp] when it comes to bringing The Bickersons to life, and he and Parker and Miss Grey could easily make an outstanding network quarter-hour out of it, but that particular brand of comedy just isn't Ed Wynn's cup of tea."

As Phil Rapp's son Paul later commented, "Virginia Grey was too pretty to play Blanche." Frances Langford, in part, agreed. "She was good as Blanche at rehearsals, but when the camera went on, she didn't want to look angry and mean like I did. And Lew had difficulty remembering all that dialogue on TV."

But the real key to The Bickerson's ultimate television failure had nothing to do with Blanche. The reality of the situation could be summed up in two words: Jackie Gleason.

The Honeymoon(ers) Is Over

Phil Rapp received many requests for John and Blanche (whoever would play them) on variety shows; the length of the skit was perfect, it required a small cast and only one set. It was also a great commercial for selling his own series. But as the old saying goes, imitation is the sincerest form of theft.

As The Bickersons became more and more familiar to a new audience, it was inevitable that someone else would latch onto the idea. On April 11, 1951, Rapp saw Gleason's show and wrote to his attorney: "The reason for this hurried note is that I saw *Cavalcade of Stars*, an hour show Friday nights on DuMont, last night. Lew Parker did a guest shot on the show and did a sketch which was supposed to be a takeoff on The Bickersons. He played his usual part and Jack Gleason was supposed to be his wife. They never referred to The Bickersons but the set they used was our Bickerson set—or a very close imitation thereof. The whole skit was played with Lew in one bed and Gleason in the other. P.S. It was lousy."

The next day, Rapp's lawyer, Jacques Leslie, wrote a letter to Abe Lastfogel of the William Morris Agency: "As you know, Phil is extremely exorcised as a result of Lew Parker's takeoff on 'The Bickersons' in the *Cavalcade of Stars* on the Dumont network last Friday night. The use of one of the principal characters in such a takeoff, as well as the use of the identical set used to televise 'The Bickersons,' and the extremely close similarity to 'The Bickersons,' is more harmful to 'The Bickersons' than the simple presentation of a mere plagiarized version thereof. From what I am told, the Parker presentation on *Cavalcade of Stars* was in extremely bad taste. You know better than anyone the importance of this property. You know too that steps must be taken to prevent any further harm to the property.

"Certainly, the New York representatives of the William Morris Agency knew that Phil objected strenuously to Parker's appearance on any guest shot. Needless to say, Phil of course objects to anyone's takeoff of 'The Bickersons.'

"Of course, because of the present negotiations with Dumont, it would be extremely unwise to commence any unpleasantness with Dumont. However, if it is possible in a pleasant way to discontinue any further showing by kinescope or otherwise, of the Parker-Bickerson sketch, it would be helpful. I think, too, that someone should talk to Parker and advise him of the poor judgement involved in the last presentation.

"I know you will do everything possible to protect 'The Bickersons.'"

Contracts at the time required the actors involved not to loan themselves out to characters or situations that would rival the show they were signing up to. However, Lew Parker was equally friendly with Gleason and Rapp both and it's doubtful that he knew he was doing anything contractually wrong. In fact, well into the '50s, Lew (and various partners) kept signing contracts with Rapp to use The Bickersons bit on numerous TV shows and nightclub appearances. But the war between Gleason and Rapp lasted nearly as long.

Other suits followed, though not to the same lengthy extent. On September 10, 1952, Richard L. Bare responded to Levoy, another of Rapp's attorneys, about Rapp's concern that Bare's short film, "So You Never Tell A Lie" was similar to the format and verbiage of The Bickersons. Bare was told that the studio usually requested a mutual exchange of scripts so that both may peruse the other's property; that is what Bare suggested. Warner Brothers was slow in acquiescing. Levoy suggested to Phil that if there was another attempt to steal The Bickersons, "we should then send a registered letter to each of the parties involved, and proceed to place it in the hands of a New York attorney for action there." The short was just one of many Bare had written and directed, and was more than likely not a Bickersons rip-off. The case was eventually dropped.

Meantime, because of the "takeoffs" and inner-industry bad blood that was beginning to flow due to the hovering litigation in the air, Phil Rapp was finding it difficult to secure final interest in his four "pilots" of Bickersons TV material. *Variety*'s November 19, 1952 issue stated, "Jack Denove, former TV production veepee at BBD&O, and Phil Rapp, writer-director, are in Gotham peddling the half-hour video series, *The Bickersons*. The pair recently completed the first four of the series, a telefilm version of the show which had a long radio career and which recently was a segment on an hour-long DuMont variety stanza. Lew Parker and Virginia Grey are starred."

Since Gleason did not heed the initial warning, and continued to run his "parodying" type of comedy, The Bickersons was news. But not necessarily the advantageous kind to its creator. On July 13, 1953, the front page of *Variety* proclaimed: Phil Rapp Warns NBC to Cease 'Plagiarism' of Bickersons on TV. A wire was sent to NBC: "You have hitherto been advised that we consider the sketch on your Hoagy Carmichael show entitled *Saturday Night Revue* involving Eddie Foy, Jr. and Sara Berner a burlesque and plagiarism of and in direct conflict with the property of Philip Rapp entitled 'The Bickersons,' with which you are fully familiar. Any such use causes considerable and inestimable damage.

"We have warned you to cease and desist. Nevertheless, we are informed that you intend to proceed flagrantly to violate the rights of Philip Rapp in the further use of same on Saturday, July 25.

"This will constitute your notice to cease and desist from the use of any material of this nature or description or which in any other way violates the property already involved in 'The Bickersons'; and you are informed that you will be held to strict accountability and damages and that Rapp will exercise such legal rights as he has in equity and in law. This notice is sent to you without waiver of any past act of violations."

Then, on August 14, 1953, *The Hollywood Reporter* told of Gordon W. Levoy and Stanley Fleishman filing a suit in Superior Court on behalf of Rapp against NBC, emcee Hoagy Carmichael, Eddie Foy, Jr., and director Sidney Miller to restrain them from using the dubious comedy sketches starring Foy on NBC's *Saturday Night Revue.*

The suit was for $750,000 actual damages and $500,000 punitive damages. Rapp estimated the value of his property at $1,500,000, especially now that he had his "four movie shorts" made at a cost of $100,000. Several networks had bid on TV rights for The Bickersons; NBC had even once took an option on it. But the value of the property wouldn't be worth much if the sketch was continued to be shown on another network, and in burlesque form at that.

Rapp had a few reliable facts on his side. The Foy sketch had been written by sketch writer Sidney Miller, who had actually played minor parts as an actor in The Bickersons. Not only did he have an intimate knowledge of The Bickersons charm, but had once requested, and been refused, rights to the series.

Back on the Gleason front, *Variety* reported on November 11, 1953 that last week Rapp filed a $2 million infringement suit in New York Federal Court against CBS, Jackie Gleason Enterprises and Jackie Gleason for his *Honeymooners*. Rapp had submitted his *It's the Bickersons* to CBS at the request of the network, who implied that it would pay "reasonable value" for the show. Instead, the skit was burlesqued in another skit (*The Honeymooners*) of roughly the same length (8 minutes).

On November 27, 1953, *Variety*'s front page reported: NBC SETTLES PHIL RAPP'S PIRACY SUIT OUT OF COURT ON 'BICKERSONS' BEEF. Though NBC paid off an undisclosed amount for their *Saturday Night Revue* infraction, the Gleason suit was still pending. Part of the agreement was that NBC would no longer run anymore "takeoffs."

Squaring off for his day in court, Jackie Gleason gave the following deposition. Notes from it are very informative when it comes to the gray area of intellectual property rights.

Court transcript

US District Court
Southern District of New York

Philip Rapp, Plaintiff against CBS, Inc., Jackie Gleason Enterprises, Inc., and Jackie Gleason, defendants.

2 p.m., Thursday, October 21, 1954, deposition taken of Jackie Gleason in room 2306 in Hotel Park-Sheraton (Jackie Gleason's residence and business), 7th Ave. and 55th St. Joseph S. Duane, notary public.

Attorneys for plaintiff: Bernard A. Grossman and Theodore R. Kupferman. For defendant: Carleton G. Eldridge, Richard G. Green and Robert A. Schulman.

Jackie Gleason, sworn by notary public, gives testimony:

Actor since age 14, records for Capitol Records, does a little writing.

On Ed Sullivan, he did his 'act' which was co-written by Gleason and writers on *The Old Gold Show* (on which he appeared as a last-minute substitute for Bobby Clark). Later, appeared on *Cavalcade of Stars*, serving as "general master of ceremonies, appearing in sketches" partly written by Gleason.

First sketch on TV called *The Honeymooners* was Oct. 5, 1951. Never done on radio. First called *Mr. and Mrs. Beast* by writer, but Gleason didn't like that and changed it to *The Honeymooners*, in October of 1951. Writers were Joe Bigelow and Harry Crane, hired by Products Advertising Corp. "I had in mind for a long time to do such a program—not a program, but a sketch—and I had often mentioned it, and the writers went to work on it and they came up with it."

"I believe that the first time I ever thought that the humor based upon two people arguing with each other might provide entertainment was when I was in Brooklyn and lived amongst these people that were continually arguing with each other." This was when he was about 15, looking for a job. "Most of my sketches are based on real-life people, and if you want to be real about a married couple, you would have to throw in a couple of arguments."

Besides Crane and Bigelow, Walter Stone, Marvin Marks and others wrote *Honeymooners* sketches on *Cavalcade*. Marks and Stone still work with Gleason on his show currently.

"Harry Crane lived in the same kind of a neighborhood that I did in Brooklyn, and he knew of these people that I was speaking to him about. He knew how they spoke and how they acted, and he more or less had a very good idea of what I wanted. I said I would like do a script about some of the people that were in my neighborhood when I was a kid—the husbands and wives who struggled, and argued with each other, who were really in love with each other, but because of some quirk of nature, they had to struggle in order to make a living."

A nine-page script of the first *Honeymooners* was produced at the deposition which "formed the basis or was used for that sketch as it was presented over DuMont in a program entitled *Cavalcade of Stars*."

Crane and Gleason also discussed "a sketch called 'The Neighborhood,' in which the characters would be the kind of people he knew about because of living in Brooklyn." Gleason lived on Chauncey Street near Saratoga, but didn't remember where Crane was from (though it was close by). The name Kramden was picked "because it didn't connote any particular race, or it doesn't mean that the couple is Irish or Jewish or German." Names were picked before the first script was written. "The Neighborhood" was to take place in front of the building where they lived, with the same kind of people.

Objection was made to having Gleason list similarities between other shows and *Honeymooners*, which would take too long. On *Cavalcade*, the corporation picked the writers, but Gleason (or his Enterprises) picked them for his show. Ralph and Alice are "facsimiles of many people; they have many people's faults and many people's graces; they are a conglomeration of many complexities."

Gleason first met Lew Parker when they appeared in *Hellzapoppin'* together in 1943. Possibly met before that, but that was the first time they worked together. Gleason remembers performing with Lew once on DuMont, as husband and wife, in which he played wife, but nothing else. Thought it was a sketch that Bert Wheeler used to do with Hank Ladd. "The fellow wanted to go to sleep and the wife kept asking him for things, or it was the other way around—I don't know. She asked him if he wanted something to eat, if he wanted something to drink, kept interrupting his sleep." Gleason saw Lew do The Bickersons on Ed Sullivan, after *Honeymooners*. Presently *The Honeymooners* sketch is part of the Gleason show, but inconsistent, runs from 12 minutes to the whole hour or not at all sometimes.

Gleason admits to having watched Sullivan/Bickersons "because my friend Parker was on it." *Honeymooners* has always been filmed at CBS at Studio 50. At DuMont it was done in the Adelphi Theatre. The kitchen/living room set was a duplicate of a home Gleason lived in.

Discussion ends at 4:10pm.

In a February 28, 1955 letter from Theodore Kupferman (another of Rapp's legal team), the attorney wrote, "I have your letter of February 17, and pursuant to your request, I called Lew Parker. He mentioned to me without my asking that he had once called Phil from the Gleason apartment.

"They are obviously trying to influence him, but I don't see what they can do to change his story in its significant aspects, and if they do and it is properly brought out, it might have a salutary effect for us on a jury.

"Parker seems to me to be a reasonable fellow, all things being considered.

"When do I get the films and other items referred to in my last letter?

"I watched the Sid Caesar show the other night, and he has a married couple along the same lines. I'm afraid everybody is doing it."

The "films and other items" referred to *It's the Bickersons* pilots and *Drene Time* scripts which Rapp had to dig out and furnish both sides to establish his claim, and a good claim it was. Many people in the business realized what was happening.

Singer Martha Stewart recalled, "My husband, Dave Shelley, was very close to Jackie Gleason, and he knew where they got *The Honeymooners* idea from. Jackie loved that show, and of course he put his own character into it in an altogether different way. Dave always used to tease him: 'I know where you got that. You got that from The Bickersons.' Jackie said, 'I did not, I made that up!' Because Jackie had to be the big creator of everything."

It's easy to see why Rapp couldn't sell his series while *The Honeymooners* was around—even the second couple (Barney and Clara) vaguely resembled Norton and Trixie. Phil continued to push his series through the end of 1954. Two days before 1955, things were looking hopeful. NBC liked the fourth Bickerson episode, but time and the court case was marching on.

A December 8, 1955 letter from Rapp's attorney Kupferman included several copies of early reviews of *The Honeymooners* (which compared it to The Bickersons). Kupferman expressed concern that they could find no copyrights for Rapp under the name "Honeymooners." He also did some background checking on *The Honeymooners'* origin:

"*The Honeymooners* was presented as a feature full-length sketch with Jackie Gleason, Art Carney, Audrey Meadows and Joyce Randolph over Channel 2 (CBS) on *The Jackie Gleason Show*, on January 16, 1954; also on the same channel on November 13, 1954; November 27, 1954; and April 16, 1955. On October 1, 1955 those four actors returned over Channel 2 for the fourth year. At present it's still on Jackie's show on Channel 2 on Saturday nights.

"CBS was considering a weekly half-hour *Honeymooners* and an audition program was to be recorded on May 6, 1954 with the four cast members and Ray Bloch's orchestra."

With $10 million in TV ad time to invest, General Motors settled on pushing its Buick car and bought *The Honeymooners* to do the job in the fall of 1955 on CBS. That kind of money left no room for the competing *It's the Bickersons*, which never did see official release.

Kupferman's associates dug up facts in which the title *Honeymooners* had been used on other programs: in 1935 there was a sustaining radio program entitled *The Honeymooners* with Grace and Eddie presented over WJZ in New York; Jane Bisher was the author of another radio series entitled *The Honeymooners* in 1940; and there were several television scripts entitled *The Honeymooners* by Angela Langford (copyright 1955) and Kaye Phyllips (also 1955). Also copyrighted was the humorous short cartoon from 1955, *The Honey Earthers* featuring script and voices by Daws Butler.

Still, Rapp hung in there, determined not to give his idea up without a fight. It was proving laborious, though the investment of time and proof was on his side. A letter written between Phil's lawyers on December 8, 1955 stated, "I cannot help but feel that even if 'bickering' per se has gone on since Adam and Eve and is the motivation in 'The Taming of the Shrew' and other significant works, that insofar as this medium is concerned (radio and television) it definitely brought a new and original format.

"P.S. I am also enclosing a copy of a report of a *Variety* item in 1948. When this occurred, Phil's attorney (at that time) called the network and asked to hear the transcription, whereupon the show [*Two Sleepy People*] was cancelled and Phil was sued. The outcome of the suit was favorable. It may be, however, that this type of proceeding would add to the proof of the establishment of The Bickersons at that time."

The next month, Jack Denove, producer of *It's the Bickersons*, said—and would so testify—that he was unable to sell the series because of the Gleason program and the pending lawsuit.

On March 27, 1956, the defendants formally requested Rapp to provide:

1. Dates of *The Honeymooners* shows which have been copied from The Bickersons.
2. Particulars of similarities between the two properties.
3. Give examples of what dialogue *The Honeymooners* was pilfering, and give the dates of the telecasts.
4. Date and provide Bickersons episodes/situations copied.
5. "Identify by name all booking, management and/or entertainment representatives that have acted on behalf of" Rapp.
6. When, where and who observed The Bickersons so that they might be copied.

These were requested within 15 days. Kinescope recordings of *The Honeymooners* were offered for study, under supervision. Tapes and specifics traded, the suit still dragged on for another two years.

In Jack O'Brian's January 2, 1958 *TViews* column in the *New York Journal-American*, the columnist thought that Gleason's "ego finally failed him" when he took The Honeymooners to a half-hour show, writing that "Ralph and Alice Kramden were his flimsiest characters." It was all right when it was a simple sketch, but he "never believed once that such a caricature of nastiness could be cured in the final moment of a sketch by the love of a good woman and the quick-decision: 'You're the greatest.'" And again, the Rapp relation crept in. "The Honeymooners was literal comedy, based on bickering; The Bickersons were its forerunner."

The case was looking bright in the Rapp camp. So bright, in fact, that on March 17, 1958, in order to assuage Kupferman's fears about having a good case, Levoy sent some cases which cited strong "implied-in-fact" contracts. Levoy felt that the strength of their winning the case lied in 1. Gleason attempting to negotiate for The Bickersons package and 2. the meetings CBS had over acquiring The Bickersons. But CBS had had enough, and urged Gleason to settle out of court. CBS paid Rapp an undisclosed sum that year to call off the suit, and Rapp, very tired from nearly a decade of argument, agreed. The bickering finally concluded.

Bickering and Pitching

Now that it looked as though The Bickersons would not have its own television series, Phil Rapp eagerly acquiesced when other venues popped up. On November 21, 1956, an AFTRA agreement was signed by him with Bellmeadows Enterprises for the services of Betty Kean and Lew Parker as John and Blanche on *The Steve Allen Show* four days later on November 25 from 8-9 p.m. for $3,000. They were such a hit that Steve asked them back for a December 9th performance on the same terms. The audiences at the Hudson Theatre loved it.

So did Lew and Betty, who signed at least one contract with Rapp on May 29, 1958, giving them permission to perform a Bickersons skit in their nightclub/café act, in which they would pay Rapp 15% of the gross for the privilege. Phil never held a grudge against Lew during the Gleason years—especially not when a sale was involved.

Even the BBC were interested in The Bickersons, but in a July 2, 1958 letter from the William Morris Agency to Rapp, "they state that there is a big obstacle to overcome if we want Parker and Kean to do the parts." Their London office stated that they could perhaps get the BBC to reconsider if "we ever change our minds and use two people the BBC suggested." Whoever these "people" were remains a mystery.

Variety's review of Parker and Kean's "socko" Bickersons at The Copacabana read: "It's about time they are rediscovered for the basic television medium from which this pioneer situation comedy stemmed." That same magazine's review of their performance in Pittsburgh raved, "Any way you look at them, Kean and Parker are on the gold standard" and that their Bickersons was "a sharp, smart slice of Rapp's typical domestic comedy, delivered by a couple of real pros." From *The New York Mirror* to the *Kansas City Star*, adulation for the act was unremitting. On December 3,

1958 they performed at the Coconut Grove in the Los Angeles' Ambassador Hotel, and on Christmas Day of that year, at the Statler Hilton in Dallas, Texas. On November 26, 1958 they took out a full-page ad in *Variety* showing off their worthy reviews.

Another magazine called The Bickersons the high point of the act at The Copacabana, comparing it favorably to the Langford/Parker series, but admitted "that nobody can fight as realistically as husband and wife." The other parts of their act involved a duet called "Everything We Do, We Do Together," an impression of Anna Magnani and Anthony Quinn, plus a parody of *My Fair Lady*.

It was announced that Lew and Betty would be shooting the pilot for a television version of The Bickersons on April 19, 1959, financed by Bernard Shubert. Screen Gems had optioned The Bickersons for a television series on October 1, 1958, paying Rapp $1,000. Once the pilot had been shot (which no longer exists) and screened (starring Parker and singer Evelyn Knight), Schubert wrote to Rapp: "No question, Phil, everyone was most enthusiastic about what could be done with the show. Unfortunately, because of the costs involved, I am afraid we would have to get some idea from you as to what the outside costs would be to produce 26 of THE BICKERSONS for TV syndication. Once you give me some idea of this, Phil, I can advise you whether or not we have any interest."

After Rapp submitted the below budget, a responding telegram wanted at least $1,500 cut off his Bickersons package price.

> Production costs – $2,850
> Evelyn Knight – $2,000
> Lew Parker – $1,500
> Music, including arrangements, leader & 8 piece orchestra – $1,150
> Cast – $500
> MRSM Bickerson – $500
> Taxes and insurance – $500
> WMA commission – $1,357
> Phil Rapp, for rights, scripts, producer, director, additional writers, assistant director and script girl – $4,575
> Total – $14,932

Bickering and Pitching • 127

Another telegram asked about reducing Parker to $1,000 net weekly, and Knight to $1,500, and also questioned what of Rapp's $4,575 could be shaved. However, even further cuts did not lead to a series.

Actually, Phil didn't need another series. He quickly found that the most lucrative part of television wasn't the show—but the commercials.

More than likely, it was Don Ameche and Frances Langford's reunion for a New York Ed Sullivan Show in March of 1958 that prompted serious sponsor interest. Now that the two original warhorses were back together and in the public eye, John and Blanche were soon bickering for Top Value Stamps in July of that year. The 60-second plot involved husband giving wife a book of Top Value Stamps for Armistice Day, "I mean our anniversary." It's what she wanted since John never gave her spending money. But he didn't do a good job licking the 1,500 stamps into the books during rush hour. At first, she wanted to get John a new shirt

for his collection. "*Collection*!? Blanche, I've only got *one* shirt. Remember—you burned up the others in the oven the day the dryer wouldn't work." Just for that insult, Blanche decided to use the stamps to buy more groceries so she could get more Top Value Stamps.

Many more commercials followed. It was an unbroken circle of success: more TV spots led to more commercial interest, which led to more guest star spots on variety series. Perry Como called Phil about Don and Frances battling on his show in early 1960. In a letter to Ameche about the Como spot, Phil admitted, "I presume  there is considerably less than a half million dollars apiece in it for all of us, but we do have a lot of fun." As owner/writer/director of the battlers, Rapp naturally received a much higher salary for all of this than the stars, but they all *did* enjoy it. Each session was a *guaranteed* laugh-getter. Don Ameche was especially grateful during the lean years of his career.

Ameche and Langford weren't always available for every piece of business, but sponsors didn't seem to mind. On March 5, 1959, D.P. Brother & Company Advertising hired Phil to write and produce four one-minute spots starring Lew Parker and Betty Kean as John and Blanche for their client, General Motors Corp. John Milton Kennedy was the announcer on three of them. Exactly two months later, D.P. Brother & Company Advertising sent a letter to Rapp proclaiming their delight at the radio commercials.

Three were recorded (called simply "Train," "Seashore" and "Neighbors") and placed in the shows *Monitor, Mitch Miller, Have Gun, Will Travel, Johnny Dollar, Suspense* and *Gunsmoke* from June 22 through July 26. They were one-minute ads on the virtues of GM's Guardian Maintenance service. Rapp received $1,500, out of which he paid the actors, though the sponsor assumed all production costs. The tracks were laid down at Universal Recorders in Hollywood on the 12 or 13th of June, 1959.

At some point, Don and Frances were set to do the following commercial, written by Rapp, for the Whaleco Fuel Company. Only a first draft was found among Rapp's papers, so it's uncertain whether the spot was ever recorded.

DON: Out of my way, Blanche—I'm late for work.

FRANCES: Work! Then why are you wearing that bedsheet?

DON: It's not a bedsheet—it's a burnoose. I got a job as doorman in a Turkish restaurant. Where's my fez?

FRANCES: Fez?

DON: That hat like a flower pot with a tassel on it!

FRANCES: Hat? I planted some okra in it...John Bickerson don't dump that fertilizer on the table!

DON: Looks better than the breakfast you left for me. Tasted awful.

FRANCES: What breakfast? I didn't make anything.

DON: You did too! In that little red bowl.

FRANCES: That was the cat's dinner!

DON: Oh, no! Live in a goat's nest and eat cat food! Where's my razor?

FRANCES: (Alarmed) John, you're not going to—

DON: I'm gonna shave! (Tap running) Blanche, there's no hot water!

FRANCES: I shut off the burner. We have to save money on the gas bills, and you can shave at the restaurant.

DON: The crummy joint doesn't even have a washroom.

FRANCES: That's weird!

DON: It's uncanny. I gotta go.

FRANCES: Wait a minute, John. I want to read this brochure to you. It says Whaleco's hot water maker will work with your heating boiler and give you all the hot water you want. What's more, it'll cut your fuel costs by as much as 60% this summer...25% all year round.

DON: What are you talking about?

FRANCES: This Whaleco. I want one, John.

DON: One what?

FRANCES: A boiler maker.

DON: Me, too! Double bourbon and easy on the beer! Bye, Blanche. (Door slam)

ANNOUNCER: Call your local Whaleco Fuel Company…
or better yet…check your local paper, this week. Low monthly payments, and it's covered for fifteen years. The hot water maker—Whaleco!

On June 24, 1959 contract for The Bickersons to appear on the *Hollywood Palace* television series.

When The Bickersons appeared on Perry Como's show in 1960, Rapp sent Goodman Ace a copy of the script on January 9th, and Como a sketch of the set, which he also wanted Ace to approve. The appearance was to be on March 15 with Don and Frances. Rapp would arrive in New York City three days earlier, as requested, to direct. In a letter to Como, Rapp wrote, "I have one small favor to ask of you, Perry. Would you please play Dr. Hersey for me? It's a lot of fun, and would add to the overall entertainment value." He did.

In some ways, the Bickersons were now more popular than ever. Though they had no steady show, like *The Honeymooners*, to plug into, they were one of the most requested novelty acts in both mediums. No wonder Columbia Records wanted them.

Recording Stars

A new audience was growing up. As radio became a music-only medium, the air was ripe for The Bickersons invading the area of comedy albums. For them, sound only still worked the best, no matter how many sight gags were thrown into the mix. So when Columbia Records, fans of the many Bickersons commercials airing at the time, asked Phil Rapp about doing an original album of the stuff, the creator jumped at it.

Rapp flew to New York on March 6, 1961 to put everything in order that would reunite the original Langford/Ameche team of Bickersons. A tentative date for recording 35 to 40 minutes worth of material at Perry Como's studio was set for June 6th and 8th of that year, to be recorded in front of a live audience. Rapp was adamant on keeping the live flavor, so that even if a line were partially obscured by laughter, the line would stay as is. Except for the fact that the production quality was better, and in stereo, it's often hard to tell the difference between the album tracks and *Old Gold Show* bits. Everyone wanted the record to be out for that Christmas, securing it a spot in the Columbia House Record Club.

The Bickersons was released in November of 1961 on the Columbia/CBS label. Don and Frances were shown arguing in their separate beds in several poses on the cover. In April of 1961 a royalty rate had been set for the record: the combined artist royalty (Ameche and Langford) was 5 cents per record, with Rapp receiving 15 cents a record for his copyrighted characters. The suggested retail price was $3.98 for the mono recording and $4.98 for the stereo version. A 45 single boasting "more from the hottest comedy record in the country!" was passed around to radio stations resulting in frequent airplay.

The record was such a hit (even ending up on airplanes), that Columbia decided to follow it up with a sequel recording. *The Bickersons Fight Back* was

Recording Stars • 135

released the following August. A compilation of both albums under the name *The Bickersons Rematch* was put out in April 1971. Phil, Don and Frances received royalties on these for years afterwards. The albums ultimately sold in the hundreds of thousands, in 37 countries, and the BMI checks (for radio play) that Rapp received were simply staggering.

Because of the colossal popularity of the albums, in 1962 Alan Spilton and Gloria Shayne wrote a song called "You Say It (But You Won't Do It)," which they sent to Phil. It was a duet for man and wife in which, like

The Bickersons, she complains that he promises to help with the chores and wants her warm embraces, but he's too tired to do anything about anything. Though it was published by Daywin Music of Beverly Hills, California, it is not known to have been recorded. Spilton was famous for co-writing "Lover Come Back," while Gloria Shayne soaked up many a co-writer's royalty for her Christmas hit "Do You Hear What I Hear?"

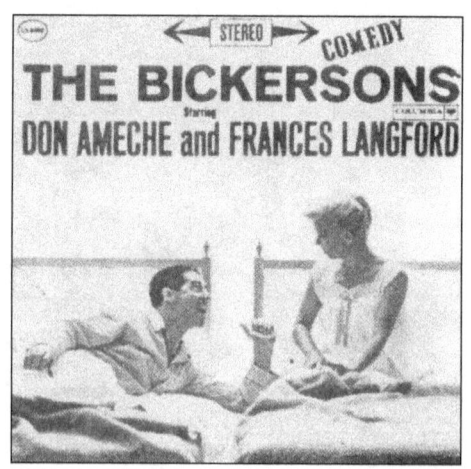

SHE: You say it,
HE: I'd take you out to a show,
SHE: but you won't do it.
HE: but I'm too tired to go.
SHE: You say it,
HE: Someday I'll teach you to drive,
SHE: but you won't do it.
HE: I'd rather stay alive.

SHE: You say you'll help me with the dishes when the dinner's thru,
HE: I'll mow the lawn and feed the cat
SHE: And do the laundry, too.
HE: I'm not Mister Clean, a washing machine or a scull'ry maid to you.

SHE: You say it,
HE: I'd do the pots and pans,
SHE: but you won't do it.
HE: But I'd get dish pan hands.

138 • The Bickersons

Phil, Don and Frances at the Columbia recording session.

SHE: You say before we go to sleep, you'd like my warm embrace.

HE: But with that grease pack on you, my lips would slip right off your face. With your hair in pins, your strapped up chins, you're straight from outer space.

SHE: You say it,

HE: O.K., I'll kiss you goodnight.

SHE: but you won't do it.

HE: Not till you turn out the light.

SHE: Your snoring and your grunting sound like two pigs in a fight

HE: I bet you'd like it better if I held my breath all night.

SHE: Say you're saving money, just to purchase me a mink.

HE: But honey, saving money's not as easy as you think.

SHE: Of course, it's hard to save it when you're spending it on drink. You say all those things but you don't do one.

HE: Some things are easier said than done.

SHE: (Speaks) Like what, John, come on, tell me. Let's see you get out of this one!

HE: (Speaks) I could tell you plenty, don't worry about me!

(Sings) You know I think you're beautiful, I love your wit and charm.

SHE: Prove what you say's the real McCoy and not a false alarm.

HE: To prove to you my love is true, I'd cut off my right arm.

SHE: You say it,

HE: (Speaks) Sure I say it,

SHE: but you won't do it.

HE: (Speaks) Sure I'll do it,

SHE: Do it now!

HE: (Speaks) You know how I hate the sight of blood.

SHE: Especially your own! (Back to start of song)

The resulting airplay and impressive record store sales fueled continued interest from PR firms and advertisers. In 1964, the Geyer/Morey/Ballard Inc. ad agency in New York requested Phil's stars for two one-minute commercials for their client, American Motors Corp. (Rambler Division):

Plot 1. John loves driving his new Rambler Classic, so is always picking up the guys in the car pool.

Plot 2. Blanche wakes John up at 4 in the morning because there's a Rambler dealer downstairs. She wants him to decide between the Rambler American, Rambler Classic or Rambler Ambassador V-8 for 1964.

Next, an agreement arrived on September 8, 1964 from Senior Enterprises on behalf of their client, the Harrison Radiator Division of General Motors, for Frances and Don to appear in six 60-second radio commercials. Rapp received $1,500 for the right to the name and securing the talent, plus first class airfare to New York City. The agency footed

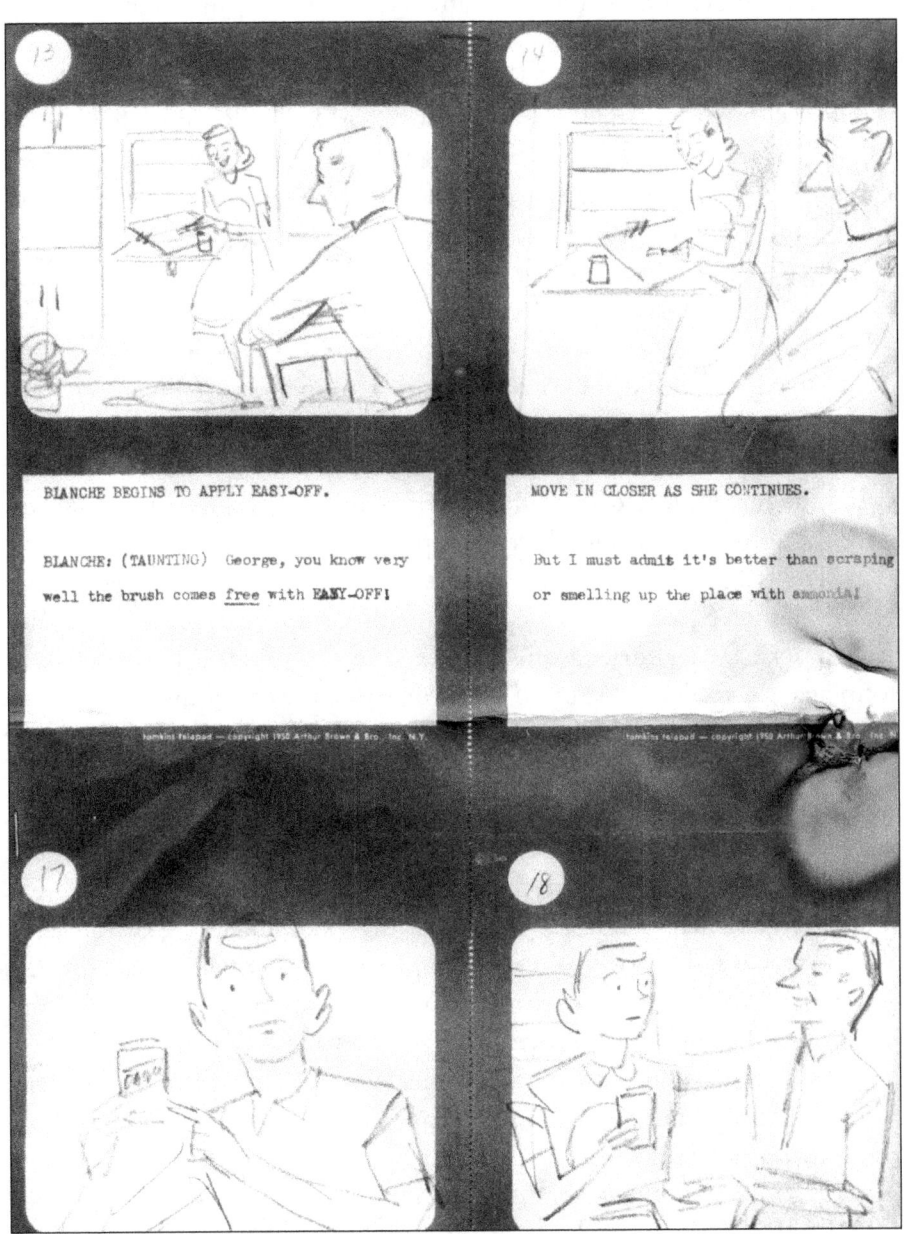

Original storyboard page of an Easy Off commercial.

all costs of production, and the broadcasts ran in the weeks of October 12 & November 9 of 1964, and January 18, June 7, July 5 and August 2 of 1965.

A year later, Campbell-Mithun, Inc., a Minneapolis, Minnesota advertising company, signed The Bickersons and Philip Rapp up for a series of 10 four-minute and thirty second "radio programs" (commercials). Lew Parker and "woman mutually acceptable" were to star after an audition program was produced. Phil was to be in complete charge (direction, casting, writing, producing), with script approval to be held by their client, old fan Top Value Enterprises, Inc. The budget of the audition program was set at $4,500, with the remaining nine commercials set at $25,500 total.

On September 6, 1966, a 60-second radio spot for Pream was approved by the ad agency. Back to cars, several 60-second plots were then devised for the D.P. Brother and Company advertising agency. Their client: again, the Harrison Radiator Division of General Motors. Some situations were thought up, but not all were scripted.

They're driving to a party. Blanche spent three hours in the beauty parlor, but keeps asking for the windows up or down to protect her hair. She wants a GM Four Season Climate Control, or she'll never speak to John again! "You say it but you won't do it!" quibbles John.

John and Blanche are driving to her mother's home. They're lovey dovey with the new GMFSCC in the car. But when Blanche finds that John didn't call Mother to tell her they're coming, all bicker breaks loose.

Blanche has made John put the cat and goldfish in the car for a trip, but she insists on bringing Marvin, their canary. "Then let him fly after us!" yells John. "Fly!" Blanche exclaims. "You know that poor little thing gets airsick."

John has fallen asleep at the wheel. He's been giving Blanche driving lessons for 12 years, but she won't take the wheel because it's too hot. John knows he'll have to break down and get a new car – with GMFSCC.

Coming back from seeing the tropical film *Under Pagan Skies*, Blanche rues their stifling car. She's also steaming because Gloria Gooseby was sitting in front of them. But she stuffed a bag of unshucked peanuts down her back, and admits that even Gloria looks good because she's got a car with GMFSCC.

Several other scripts were assembled and recorded, including:

ANNCR: And now – Don Ameche and Frances Langford as "The Bickersons."

Don, Frances and Bing Crosby on TV.

JOHN: (GIRDING FOR BATTLE) I knew it! The new car's gone again! OK, Blanche, which one of your relatives borrowed it this time?

BLANCHE: (SPOILING FOR THE FRAY) My mother!

JOHN: I see! Lady MacBeth rides again!

BLANCHE: It's your own fault, John! When you got that new car with General Motors Four-Season Climate Control, you had to hold a press conference! Kept bragging it up about how much fresher you feel at the wheel with conditioned air…no problems with pollen or excess humidity. Temperature's always just right—every day of the year. Clothes clean and neat.

JOHN: For years she avoids me like a plague!…Now I get a car with GM Harrison Climate Control and suddenly I'm "Mister Wonderful!" When'll the Juggernaut be back?

BLANCHE: If you mean "mother," she's returning day after tomorrow.

JOHN: I guess now the only time I can depend on having the car to myself is Halloween.

BLANCHE: Halloween?

JOHN: That's the night she rides her broomstick!

ANNCR: Try Four-Season Climate Control…or Cadillac Comfort Control. Enjoy wonderful weather wherever you drive…the ideal temperature inside your car every day of the year. GM Harrison Four-Season Climate Control is available on Chevrolets, Pontiacs, Oldsmobiles and Buicks—most of the smaller-size models, too. Ask for a demonstration at your General Motors Dealers.

While commercials mounted, the occasional television appearance still popped up. On May 13, 1967, Don and Frances appeared as The Bickersons on ABC's *Hollywood Palace*. Frances was interviewed after the show (which involved Blanche spending her tonsillectomy money on clothes, then pretending she couldn't talk): "I wouldn't think of doing The Bickersons unless Phil was around to direct it, even if it's one of our old routines. It's the timing and everything he puts into it that makes us so real and funny." During the rehearsal for this taping, Rapp had Don and Frances drilling their lines in a corner of the theatre lobby. Overhearing the violent quarreling of the comic dialogue, one passing woman called the police, which Phil Rapp considered a great compliment.

That reality made John and Blanche ripe for yet another adventure. Conquering the legitimate stage.

Match Please, Darling

In 1967, The Bickersons found a new venue for their squabbles: The stage. Co-author Joel Rapp tells the origin of this miracle in a promotional piece he wrote at the time:

THE RAPP WRITING TEAM CLOSES GENERATION GAP
by Joel Rapp

In the entire history of the American theater, only one play has ever been written by a father-son scripting team, and, as the son half of the aforementioned twosome, I am in an excellent position to tell you why!

The play is *Match Please, Darling*, currently at the Coronet Theater; the father-son writing tandem is my dad, Philip Rapp, and I, and the historic venture began eight months ago.

I had driven up to my father's palatial Beverly Hills manse, prepared for a conversation I knew to be inevitable; to wit, borrowing money. I winced as my father's words spilled out:

"Son, do you suppose you might lend me a few dollars until next Wednesday?"

I hesitated. "What about the twenty you already owe me, Dad?"

"I can't pay you this week," he said, sheepishly.

"That's what you told me last week!"

"Well," he bellowed, "I kept my word, didn't I???"

With a resigned sigh, I peeled a $20 bill off my unemployment booty, then looked my father squarely in the eye.

"Dad," I said, "I just don't understand it. How can a man who lives in Beverly Hills, drives a brand new Cadillac, belongs to the Hillcrest Country Club and plays 18 holes of golf every day be broke all the time?"

My father shook his head. "Stupid kid."

"Dad," I said, ever so tentatively, "you're one of the most important comedy writers in show business. Maybe if you cut out just a few holes of golf and accepted a job..."

I took a deep breath. I was about to suggest something that'd been on my mind for months.

"Pop, look. I know you don't want to write for TV or pictures anymore, but..."—I dreaded the reaction—"...How would you like to write a play with me?"

"After all," I continued, selling hard, "I'm an established writer. Says so right on my unemployment booklet. And I've got this great idea about a man and his wife whose marriage is..."

"Laddy-buck," he interrupted, "you must be out of your mind! You been smoking papayas or something? How can you, a mere TV comedy writer, dare hope to collaborate with a man who..."

"Yeah, yeah. A man who created Baby Snooks, a man who wrote six hilarious Danny Kaye movies, a man who..."

"No, no. A man who likes to play golf every day!"

I gulped with shame. "Sorry, Pop."

"That's OK, Son. But as long as you're listing my credits, let's not forget the most gratifying of all." He picked up a record album with a picture of Don Ameche and Frances Langford on the front. "The celebrated Batting Bickersons," he beamed, reading from the liner notes, "created by Philip Rapp and beloved to radio listeners, TV audiences, and now..."

"And now—theater-goers!"

He turned slowly. "What did you say?"

"That's the rest of my idea, Dad! I figured we could take my play plot and make the man and wife John and Blanche Bickerson! That way we could..." I stopped cold. I'd never seen him so angry.

"Every line of every routine I've ever written for John and Blanche Bickerson has my blood on it! I've sweated and slaved to invent these priceless jokes from whole cloth! How dare you suggest I share the fruit of my great comedy creation with some punk kid off the streets??"

"Punk kid off...But I'm your *son*!"

"You're no son of mine!" he said, holding out my $20 bill disdainfully. Just then, my mother walked in and plucked it from his hand.

"Hey, where do you think you're going with that? I need that money," Pop whimpered. "I'm all out of bourbon."

My mother whirled, furious. "That's why we never have any money," she said. "You've made millions and you throw every penny away on your precious bourbon."

"Now don't go making me an alcoholic!" shouted Papa. "The only reason I use bourbon is because Dr. Hersey prescribed it. He said I'd calm down if I took a jigger of bourbon and two aspirins every night."

"You're six months behind on the aspirin and two years ahead on the bourbon!"

"Well," said my father defensively, "aspirin gives me a headache!"

As mother shook her head and left the room, Dad ran excitedly to his steam-driven typewriter and began pounding the keys furiously.

"What are you doing?" I asked.

"Didn't you hear what just happened, kid? What a great routine for the Bickersons!"

"So!" I said. "You sweat blood to think up those routines, huh? Every word is painfully invented, huh? Well, the truth is finally out!"

"Son, please..."

"A writer, are you? You're nothing but a reporter!"

Dad licked his lips nervously. "Look, boy, that may be true, but it's not the kind of thing I'd like to have get out. I mean, there's my image as a comedy genius to consider..."

I straightened up and lit a cigarette, as Dad looked at me pleadingly.

"You wouldn't tell anybody...would you...?"

"Not a word," I said, exhaling a cloud of smoke. "If you'll agree to write the play with me."

The next morning we started blocking Act I. I was alive with anticipation, for the prospect of working with a genuine master of comedy was exciting. I soon learned, however, that collaborating with one's father would not be all peaches and cream. I arrived at this conclusion the first time I suggested one of my jokes was funnier than one of his.

His eyes narrowed. "What did you say?"

"I said I think my joke in this scene is better than yours."

"You really think so?" he asked, quietly.

I nodded.

"All right, son." Then suddenly, "Go to your room!"

"But Dad..."

"I said go to your room!"

I sighed resignedly. "I lost my head, Pop. Your joke is better than mine, no doubt about it."

"That's a good boy," he beamed, and our first crisis was over.

And so it went. His jokes were always better than mine, either under the threat of bed without dinner or two weeks without my allowance or other things equally terrifying to a 33-year-old man with a wife and two children.

Of course, there were other problems. Like the conflict between my father's era and my own.

The most amusing example of this occurred during the construction of what turned out to be the show's biggest laugh, where John Bickerson is alone in his apartment in his pajamas with a sexily attired Playboy Bunny. It's all perfectly innocent, but you can imagine John's embarrassment as Blanche comes in and sees her husband in bed with a voluptuous Playboy Bunny seated on the edge. The Bunny stands up, John jumps out of bed guiltily, and the audience roars. After the first preview of the show, my father said, "Son, I've got an inspiration! A great line for John."

"What is it?" I asked.

Joel and Phil Rapp

"He turns to the Bunny," said my father, "and says, 'A package of Wings, please.'"

I stared. "A package of what?"

"Wings, you dum-dum! Cigarettes! Don't you get the joke?"

"Oh," I said, starting to chuckle. "Hey, that *is* funny! But we better not make it Wings, Pop. We better make it a more modern brand…like say…a package of Marlboros …?"

Grudgingly, he acceded, and just as I figured, every night when John Bickerson asks for a package of Marlboros, the house comes down. (The funniest part is, my father still thinks it's his joke!)

Anyway, we struggled for nearly five months, and finally approached the end of the play. All we needed was one more Bickerson routine. As we sat in Dad's den vainly searching, my mother came in, waving a bank book.

"Philip," she said, "why did you withdraw $200 from our savings account?"

"I used it to pay the first premium on a $10,000 life insurance policy," said Dad, rather proudly.

"What??" My mother scowled. "You selfish beast! Squandering all that money on a life insurance policy! Always thinking of yourself!"

The *Match Please, Darling* set.

"Thinking of *myself?*" His eyes were wide with disbelief. "When I die, you get the $10,000!"

"You know you have no intention of dying!" screamed Mama. "You only did it to tantalize me!"

My father turned purple. "I'll drop dead in the morning!"

"You say it but you won't do it!"

And with that, Mama stormed out of the room. Slowly, the rage left my father's face, a beatific smile took its place and he turned.

"Son, did you hear that?"

I was already at the typewriter. "I heard, Pop, and I promise I won't tell a soul you didn't make it up!"

Well, now the play is running nightly to what I can modestly report to be enormous audience approval. I should be thrilled that my dream of writing a play with Dad has been realized, but sad to say I've discovered that a little theater production in Hollywood isn't exactly a bed of roses.

From a sleep-till-noon, $50,000-a-year TV writer, I've suddenly been transformed into an up-at-7 ticket-seller, theater sweeper, coffeemaker and actor. That's right, actor. The producers of *Match Please, Darling*, in a fit of irrationality, suddenly decided I would be perfect in the role of John Bickerson's next door neighbor and best friend.

I must admit I'm rather enjoying that part of it. All except for a rather tense moment on the first day of rehearsal. I read a line in a manner I thought extremely funny when suddenly the director bellowed: "No, no, you idiot, that's all wrong! It'll never get a laugh that way!"

"But, sir," I began to protest.

"Listen, kid," said the director, menacingly. "Either you read this line my way or else!"

My shoulders sagged and I nodded.

"Yes, Dad. Anything you say."

I'll be damned if I'm going to suffer through another night without my milk and cookies!

As the only official Bickersons play, *Match Please, Darling* gained much media attention. Joel explains: "Needless to say, the [above] piece for the *L.A. Times*, was written tongue-in-cheek, a satirical look at the travails of a son working with his legendary father. And yes, of course, using the jokes from the play was simply part of the tone of the piece. No, those conversations with my father never really occurred, at least not in the way I wrote about them. The closest thing to the 'truth' in the piece about the jokes was the anecdote about my father and my discussion over the cigarette joke. That really did happen!

"It is also true that the writing of the play came about the way I described it. Dad—lonely, unoccupied, etc., me—seizing the idea of writing a play with the Bickersons as the central characters. It took me a couple of weeks to convince him to sit down and do it with me—I think the turning point came when I got a pretty good job offer and told Dad it was time to fish or cut bait. I'd pass on the job if he'd get started with me on the play. The outcome, of course, is history.

"I don't remember how long it took to write *Match Please, Darling*—a couple of months, I'd guess—but most of it was written with Dad sitting at his steam-driven, old-fashioned typewriter (what the heck, he started his writing career with a chisel and some stone!), pecking away with two fingers faster than most people can type with both hands, while I paced the floor, smoked, and added my two cents whenever I felt like it. Dad was the ultimate 'editor' but it was a true collaboration."

Oddly, rather than inserting the usual comic foils (Mel & Louis Shaw or Leo & Gloria Gooseby), *MPD* invented the Trowels, best described in the play's character descriptions:

HARVEY JACOBSON: A divorce lawyer. Middle thirties, attractive, witty, good dresser—but like some people who are hard on shoes, Harvey is hard on money. [A version of the Barney role]

BLANCHE BICKERSON: Wife of:

Whitney Blake, Carol Thompson, and Josh Bryant.

JOHN BICKERSON: Everybody knows him.

TEDDY: Doorman—elevator operator of the apartment house where the Bickersons and Harvey reside. About fifty.

BIRDIE TROWEL: Attractive matron until she opens her mouth. Tactless, voluble.

HERB TROWEL: Birdie's fawning consort. Continental manners, sickening attention to Birdie's tiniest whim, but not altogether unlikable.

ADELAIDE: A Bunny from the Playboy Club.

The play takes place "today" in the Bickersons' fifth floor apartment on the East River of New York. They have lived in Apt. 501 for 11 years, John having been there 2 years before marrying Blanche. As the opening description states, "Blanche is not a shrew. She loves her impecunious husband and is rather tolerant of his peccadilloes, although prone to magnify them in the heat of argument. But with the superb illogic of every married woman, she wants a better and more luxurious life."

The only neighbor (on the same floor) they see is divorce lawyer Harvey, though Blanche's best friends are the Trowels who repose in the swanky penthouse. John loathes their existence as he's always being compared to Herb and the inane way he dotes on his wife, Birdie, whenever she withdraws a cigarette and asks him for a "match please, darling."

It's the Bickersons' Steel anniversary (the 11th), and the Trowels are having the doorman lay out paper plates and cups for the festive occasion in the top-floor pad. After a long-suffering day trying to sell cemetery plots, the last thing John Bickerson wants to do is party with loathsome people. Business is bad. In three weeks he's only managed to sell one thing—a crypt to The Mysticrucians, a fraternal order of six Friars who bought it as a retreat, "for meditation and prayer. They live in complete silence, Blanche, and I'm thinking of joining them!"

The Trowels come down to give the Bickersons their anniversary present: a portrait of themselves. It's revolting (Herb is kissing Birdie's hand), but Blanche wants John to take down "the world's only composite picture of General Grant and Dean Martin" and hang it above the bar. After Blanche leaves, he hangs it in the bathroom over the toilet. When John gets a call from the Mysticrucians, who have his check ready, he scampers out in pajamas, leaving Harvey the opportunity to call his bookie in Las Vegas. The voluptuous Playboy Bunny Adelaide Rogers arrives looking for John, but Harvey coaxes her in. "Put down your bundles and relax." "Bundles?" she asks. "I don't have any bundles." She breaks down crying that John—the only man she's ever been with—is the father of her child, flooring the disbelieving Harvey. John arrives and, via the bathroom portrait, it's discovered that Herb is the man; he's been using John's name, every Wednesday night (the only time he leaves his wife for even a minute) to "play handball at the club." John feels so great about being able to upset Blanche's vision of the Trowels' wedded bliss, he beams as he removes Dean Martin from over the bar.

Act 2. John is missing and the anniversary party's in full swing. He finally comes in, strips off and crawls into bed. He's been in jail since 4 in the morning.

Josh Bryant and Whitney Blake.

The Mysticrucians were really bookmakers with nine phones and were taking bets like crazy when the cops (dressed as women) raided the tomb. Adelaide, now dressed in her Bunny costume in order to have a showdown with Herb (at Harvey's insistence), has changed her mind about suing Herb and just wants to go back home and marry Gaylord who runs a chicken farm and still loves her. Blanche returns to find John consoling Adelaide. When she again holds Herb up as the perfect husband, John lets loose with the truth, which Blanche doesn't believe. When Adelaide fails to confirm the affair, Blanche is coaxed by Birdie into saying she wants a divorce. Blanche leaves to stay with the Trowels, and though John is happy about being a bachelor again, he just can't seem to get to sleep. He needs to be nagged.

Act 3. Five days later, the apartment is a mess and John is miserable. He's worse off when he gets the phone bill—$37 in calls to Las Vegas. Harvey makes the mistake of entering at that moment to tell John he's handling Blanche's divorce. He relents after admitting that he's married Adelaide; she wasn't pregnant, it was a 24-hour flu, but now she *is* expecting a child. Meantime, Herb, fed up with fawning over his wife, admits the affair (and the 15 others before her), and tells everyone that he and Birdie aren't really married. Birdie, either loving him greatly or not wanting to lose face at the scandal, pleads with Herb so much that their roles become reversed. *She* waits on *him*. Blanche is upset that her paragon of husbandhood is false and comes back to John. They are happy for exactly two minutes, until John reveals the auto-bridge (cards) set he bought her for her anniversary present set him back a whole seven bucks. They argue as the Curtain Falls.

"Soon after we finished the play," recalled Joel, "I got a call from Roger Corman asking me to come with him to Europe to supervise production of a picture, leaving Dad to try to sell the play. Broadway was the ultimate goal, of course, but we needed to go first for a local production to see how it worked. The only request I made was that if Dad sold it while I was away he'd save the part of Harvey Jacobson for me to play, although I'd really never done much acting. I'd written the Harvey part specifically for me and was both elated and disappointed when Dad called me in Amsterdam to tell me the play was financed, we would open at the Coronet Theater, and he had to begin casting ASAP. I wasn't going to be done for another four or five weeks, so we agreed the part of Harvey would go to somebody else.

"By the time I returned home the play was mounted and rehearsals were under way, Dad having decided to direct the play himself. The part

Match Please, Darling • 159

Joel Rapp, Del Moore, and Josh Bryant.

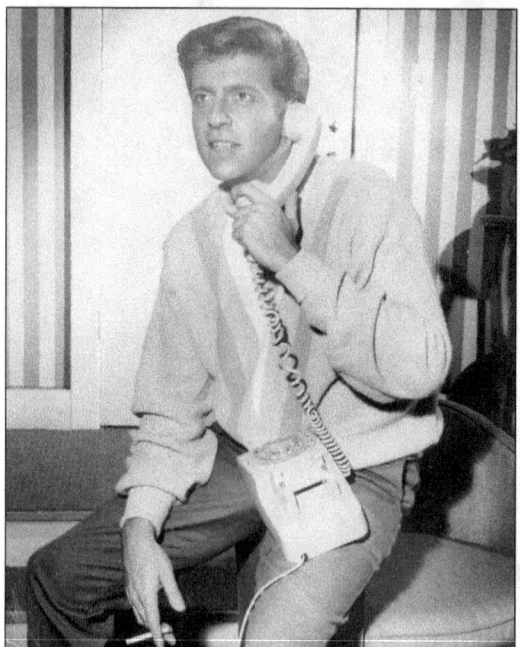

Joel Rapp, Del Moore, and Josh Bryant.

Joel Rapp.

of Harvey had gone to an actor/comic named Marc London, who was okay, but I felt not as good as I would have been.

"We opened a few weeks later to mostly good reviews (all Dad's directing reviews were excellent), the *L.A. Times* being the lone dissenter, admitting the play was funny but 'was too lightweight for Broadway.' About three weeks went by during which time we did quite a bit of rewriting (this was our 'New Haven' tryout as far as we were concerned), and then we made some cast changes: Abby Dalton, who played Blanche, got a job in a TV series and had to leave. She was replaced by Whitney Blake, who started out playing Birdie, and who wanted to play Blanche so bad she actually cut her long blonde hair very short to satisfy one little joke in the play, a joke that could have been cut with much less effort than cutting her hair.

"Anyway, she got the part and was terrific. Joey Forman, a comic/actor who played John and was just perfect, got a call to come work in Vegas, so we replaced him with a young actor named Josh Bryant who was very, very good. Del Moore, Jerry Lewis' eternal sidekick, was just great as Herb, as was veteran character actor Jack Bernardi as the Doorman. Brenda Benet (who later married Bill Bixby of the *Hulk* and then, sadly, committed suicide some years later) was our first Playboy Bunny; when she got a better gig, we put in a girl named Carol Thompson, who was just great. It's amazing how many beautiful young girls we auditioned, and amazing how many of those were really quite good. And finally, Marc London was let go and I took over the role of Harvey, as I had wanted from the beginning.

"At that point I called Sylvie Drake at the *Times*, who had reviewed the play, and she agreed to come back and have another look, what with all the changes in place. The result—she wrote a much nicer review, especially praising the cast changes, but still did not feel the show was Broadway-bound.

"Eleven weeks went by and we played nightly to half-full or three-quarter-full houses, enough to break-even every week, while we were trying to make a deal for Broadway or even a Vegas version. When nothing materialized, my father decided to close the show down. No sense knocking our brains out every night and only breaking even. But it was sure fun while it lasted!"

The play premiered at the Coronet Theatre in Los Angeles on September 20, 1967.

Reviews for the show were mixed, but overall positive. Dorothy H. Rochmis of *The Jewish Voice* newspaper wrote: "It's light, bright and funny despite several sluggish spots and several fluffs in concept and design." She wondered how, if the Bickersons are so poor, with John not selling any cemetery plots, the couple could afford to live in a fancy apartment. Incorporating the "new apartment" routine, in which John is forced into being the janitor, may have solved this "plot hole." There were other directorial quirks she objected to, but she found Joey Forman and Abby Dalton as John and Blanche remarkably well-cast. "The show is loaded with laughs, with bright, inventive actors and with no—repeat no—message."

Variety was highly complimentary, calling it "a rollicking marital farce. Considerable rewrite is necessary if it is to become full bloom, but what appears has the making of a frothy comedy which could encompass a wide audience in its stride." While *Variety* thought the first act dragged a little, it reported the "present outing is long on laugh lines" and called it "a hilarious tour de force."

The Hollywood Reporter regarded it as "some of the fleetest foolishness I have ever observed. Philip Rapp's direction is bright and inventive." Barney Glazer's *In Hollywood* column stated "it's the most pleasurable evening I've spent since I dreamed that Richard Burton left Liz Taylor on my doorstep and ran off with Eddie Fisher. Some of the lines date back before Achilles was a heel..." Staff writer for the *Herald-Examiner*, Richard Baxter, summed it up in a feature article he wrote on Phil Rapp and the play, calling the play quite changed (cast and script) from its first contour, but that it "is not a theatrical coup. On this critics have agreed, and not wholly without reason. It is not what you would call a moving piece, and the characters are less than three-dimensional. It's just an old-fashioned comedy, a funny-line play."

Margaret Harford of the *L.A. Times* was downright mean, calling the plot one long argument, likening it to a "precocious child—cute but tedious. Life with the battling Bickerons is as broad and oversimplified as ever. They are still comic strip characters like Maggie and Jiggs and their marital jousting is as predictable as most of the jokes."

Perhaps the timing was wrong. It was the season after the Summer of Love, when many items, especially in the theater, were so politically charged that *not* to say something "significant" did not "look good." Phil himself thought the critics were being overly sensitive to that component. "We wrote this purely to entertain," he told a reporter, "to produce laughter. We never considered it a gem. When you write a drama, you can't gauge it right away. But when you write a comedy, you have an audible response. They laugh, or they don't." He also humbly admitted it was

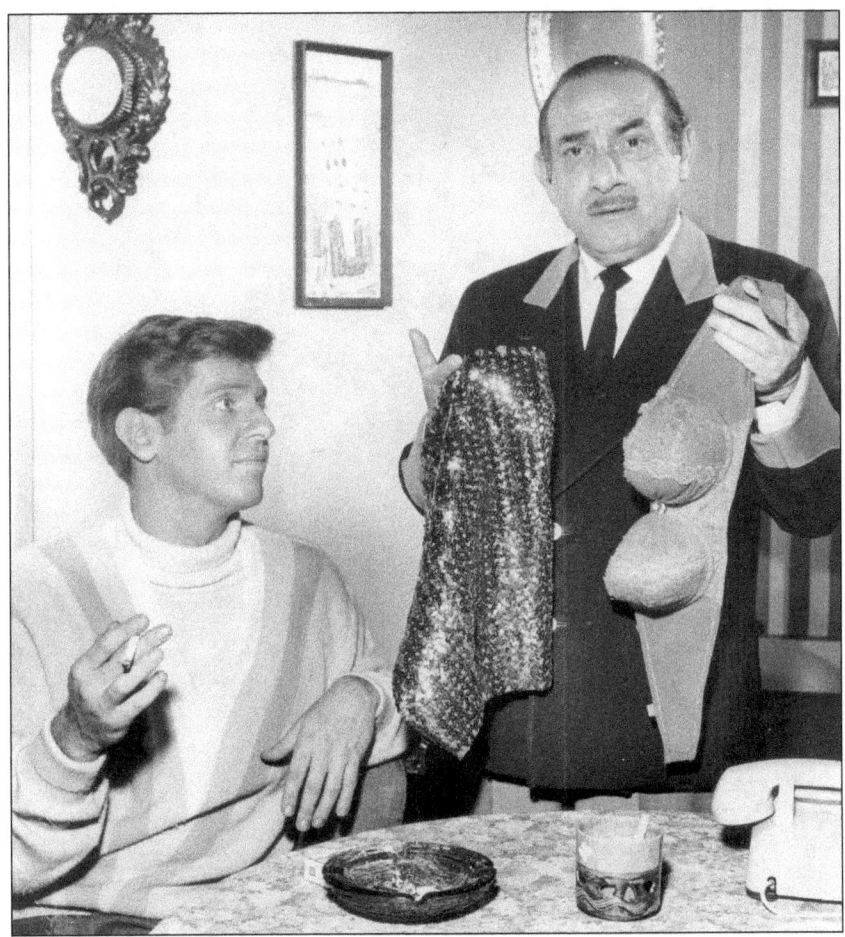

Joel Rapp and Jack Bernardi.

the first play he'd written that no one had walked out on.

Early notices before rehearsals were to start had the title as *The Honeymoon Is Over*, stating that Lew Parker and Helen Greco would star. Perhaps Lew didn't think *That Girl*, the television series he had begun the previous year, would last, or it was just wishful reporting, but Parker never even began rehearsals on the play. When cast changes were reported (Whitney Blake replacing Abby Dalton, for instance), it was revealed that the play was originally written for Don Ameche to play John.

When Whitney Blake first joined the cast, she was perplexed at Phil's complete pride in his characters, stating that the Bickersons were his legacy. She thought the Bickersons were too mean, that they needed more heart, to which Rapp replied, "There are no happy marriages. Marriage is for women.

Del Moore.

It's a disaster for men. I don't consider that the Bickersons fight. It's all a result of frustration, confusion and exhaustion. The Bickersons don't mean what they say. When they argue, they aren't fighting. Life would be pretty dull without any arguments, anyway."

Though Gloria Gooseby wasn't there to give sexual tension to the fights, the Bunny was. It was smart bit of casting that never failed to elicit reviewer response, most papers singling out the character for her beauty. It was the swingin' '60s, after all. The Rapps had to secure permission from Playboy Clubs to use their Bunny. Costuming for the well-endowed figure was supervised and furnished, therefore, by the Los Angeles Playboy Club.

In a January 12, 1968 letter from Frances Langford's husband, Ralph Evinrude, he expressed interest in investing in *Match Please, Darling*.

Lynn Wood.

Frances would invest $5000 and Evinrude $5000, with an understanding that the show would play on the road and wind up in New York. The investment would be a limited partnership deal with Phil as general partner and the investors as limited partners, but when the tour failed to materialize, so, too, did the partnership.

Joel Rapp: "A couple of interesting sidebars: Pranks abounded among the cast, especially Del [Moore]. One night I opened a closet door per the script and there stood Del, unseen by the audience, stark naked! It was all I could do to go on with the show. And there was a scene near the end of the third act with Del and Josh [Bryant] where we were supposed to be drunk, and I guess that almost every night half of that scene was ad-libbed! My father didn't like it, but audiences didn't seem to care, so we kept it up until the end of the run. By the way, the characters of Herb and Birdie were modeled after a pair of my parents' best friends—he was an artist at Disney (truly great) and she ran a chain of stores she inherited from her family. Mel Shaw (the artist) was very much like Herb Trowel, always jumping to light Louise's cigarettes, etc., to preserve his status as her husband. They both loved the play and were happily married for many years.

"Interestingly, Joey Bishop was having a 'thing' with Abby Dalton at that time and used to come backstage two or three nights a week when Abby was there, and Jerry Lewis, Del's best friend, was backstage very frequently, causing endless, but usually funny, disruptions.

"There was one moment in the play where Joey (John) phoned a prospect, trying to sell him a cemetery plot, flipping on a tape recorder playing solemn music as he began his spiel. Every night when he hit the button on the tape recorder and solemn music came, the house fell in—at least a 30-second laugh. Then, when Joey left and Josh took over, the first night Josh got all the laughs—but that cemetery-plot bit got nothing. I mean, barely a snicker. We couldn't figure out what was wrong. That laugh had come every night for weeks. For the next two nights, Dad and I watched closely to see what Josh was doing or saying differently from Joey, but could spot nothing. Finally, we called Joey in Vegas and asked him to walk us through exactly what he had been doing. It turned out he'd picked up the phone on a different line from the one Josh was doing it, and sure enough, when Josh changed that one little teeny piece of business, the laugh came again and stayed for the run of the play. It was quite a lesson for me to see how from such little things a comedy can rise or fall.

"There was a silver lining to our closing the play. At the time we shut down I was 'between wives,' living a somewhat vagabond life. I had one of those transient, bachelor-type apartments which I didn't really want to decorate. So I asked for and received the furniture from the set of the play (beds, a couch, a kitchen table and chairs, a couple of lamps) and frankly it looked pretty darn good! Waste not, want not, I always say!

"All in all, *Match Please, Darling* was one of the most wonderful experiences of my life from beginning to end."

And More Commercials

John and Blanche Bickerson may not have shouted their way into Broadway hearts, but they certainly kept screaming through radio speakers. It seems as though they had every kind of sponsor imaginable. They even sold shirts, as demonstrated by this April 28, 1969 script for Textile Improvements Limited.

DON: Blanche...do you mind if I get dressed and go to work?

FRANCES: I don't care what you do...get dressed.

DON: I will as soon as you finish wiping the dishes with my shirt.

FRANCES: Well, you shouldn't have hung it in the towel rack.

ANCR: Maybe you don't remember when The Bickersons was one of radio's top shows...or bobby socks... or milk at 10 cents a quart.

But as far back as you can remember, the Sanforized label was your assurance of shrink resistance in any garment.

Today, there's a new label...Sanforized-Plus-2 on permanent press garments that meets our standards of shrink resistance.

Sanforized-Plus-2 on slacks or shirts is your assurance they won't shrink out of fit...whether laundered commercially or at home...line or tumble dried.

DON:	And stop using my pants for a pot holder.
FRANCES:	Well, that's what you use them for.
DON:	Just leave my pot out of this.
ANNCR:	Look for the Sanforized-Plus-2 label when you buy B.V.D. shirts.

    The above was actually achieved by extracting parts of the first CBS album. Each commercial was broadcast for 13 weeks, during 1969, beginning in May, in Canada only, for a total of $650. Textile Improvements, LTD. liked the spots so much, on January 12, 1971 Rapp again received $500 for writing three new Bickersons commercials, with an additional $3,500 earmarked to produce them.

17/71	YOUNG & RUBICAM, LTD.	TEXTILE IMPROVEMENTS LIMITED Sanforized "The Bickersons #2" 71R-33-8

BLANCHE: John Bickerson, I've simply got to have a new dress.

JOHN: I can't give you any money this week, Blanche.

BLANCHE: That's what you said last week!

JOHN: Well, I kept my word, didn't I? You can't keep on squandering money on new dresses!

BLANCHE: Squandering money! All I've got is that black sheath - and I got that for a ridiculous figure.

JOHN: Can I help it if you've got a ridiculous figure?

BLANCHE: ~~Talk about squandering~~! If there's ever an extra dollar in the house you spend it on yourself.

JOHN: Me? I never spend a penny on myself. My only bathing suit has a hole in the knee! I've been sewing collars on your old bloomers and wearing 'em for shirts! I deny myself everything!

BLANCHE: You bought a tiepin yesterday!

JOHN: What tiepin! That was a hypodermic needle - I've been selling my blood!

ANNCR: Maybe the Bickersons wouldn't have had so much to bicker about if permanent press garments had been available. Or would they? Some permanent press garments CAN and DO shrink. But not when they carry the Sanforized-Plus-2 trademark. Sanforized-Plus-2 on any garment is your complete assurance that it will not shrink out of shape or fit, no matter how

- 2 -

TEXTILE IMPROVEMENTS
LIMITED
Sanforized
"The Bickersons #2"

71R-33-8

it's laundered.

BLANCHE: I walk around in rags and I'm ashamed to be seen on the street. Everyplace I go people point at me and say "There goes Bickerson's wife - look how she dresses!"

JOHN: Look how I dress - and I'm Bickerson. Outta my way, Blanche.

ANNCR: Look for the Sanforized-Plus-2 label when you buy Arrow shirts.

```
Feb.17/71          YOUNG & RUBICAM, LTD.        TEXTILE IMPROVEMENTS
                                                LIMITED
                                                Sanforized
                                                "The Bickersons #3"

                                                71R-33-8
```

JOHN: BLANCHE! Come here and look at this shirt - it's got no buttons on it!

BLANCHE: Stop yelling, John Bickerson. Just stick a strip of scotch tape down the front and nobody'll notice it.

JOHN: Nobody'll notice it! I swear, Blanche —

BLANCHE: Oh, just eat your breakfast and get off to work. There.

JOHN: What is THAT!

BLANCHE: It's pickled frog's legs and yoghurt. I got the recipe from my mother.

JOHN: It looks like your mother. I don't wanna eat it, Blanche. You and your crazy cooking. Yesterday you tried to give me that rhubarb pie.

BLANCHE: What was the matter with it?

JOHN: Who ever heard of a pie two feet long?

BLANCHE: Well, I couldn't get any shorter rhubarb!

ANNCR: Pity the poor Bickersons. They didn't know how easy life could be with unshrinkable, permanent press shirts. But even today, some permanent press garments CAN and DO shrink...unless they carry the Sanforized-Plus-2 trademark. Sanforized-Plus-2 on any garment is your assurance that it will not shrink out of shape or fit, no matter how it's laundered.

```
                        - 2 -                TEXTILE IMPROVEMENTS
                                             LIMITED
                                             Sanforized
                                             "The Bickersons #3"

                                             71R-33-8
```

BLANCHE: You always complain about my cooking. You hate everything I cook.

JOHN: Blanche, I don't hate it - I just don't understand it!

BLANCHE: You hate it!

JOHN: I tell you I don't hate it - don't I eat everything you make?

BLANCHE: Then why do you always get ptomaine poisoning?

JOHN: Goodbye, Blanche!

ANNCR: Look for the Sanforized-Plus-2 label when you buy B.V.D. shirts.

Very Animated

On February 24, 1970, it was announced in *Film/TV Daily* that KFI Films Inc. would produce a weekly syndicated Bickersons cartoon series. Stephen Krantz, president of KFI, made the announcement that Phil Rapp would write and direct the soundtrack. Production would begin immediately with Ralph Bakshi as executive producer.

For a pilot, Phil handed in one of his surefire-laugh scripts, actually the one used for the pilot of the ill-fated 1948 half-hour series (John meets nephew on the train). Once that was approved as the basis for the story, Phil set to writing an expanded version, for the many sight gags necessary for a cartoon show. Krantz Films wanted even more visual jokes than was handed in; most involving John dealing with his bowling balls on the train and trying to sell them door-to-door. The studio mentioned one possible ending that was never scripted or storyboarded: "After John takes Harvey home by mistake, I think Little Darling [the "nephew" of this version] could notice that her father is missing. This could be developed into a scene with the same policeman with Little Darling announcing that her father has been kidnapped by John Bickerson, the same man who pulled a knife on her and stole her bubble gum. Of course, this whole situation should have a happy ending after the policeman is mollified, and as John is about to fall asleep to catch the plane, Little Darling wakes him up and asks him to tell her a story. He complies reluctantly, and she says, snuggling up

to him, something like, 'You tell very nice stories, Uncle John.'"

Once the storyboards were complete, aside from a few comments about gags, Phil was happy with what he saw. But he did suggest that friend Harvey should not have a mustache since John Bickerson has one; and that the Bickersons *must* be in twin beds, not in a double bed.

Oddly, another animation script was prepared using some of the same material (ending with bringing Barney back home through the dead of night), but this Halloween episode did contain elements of a Baby Snooks bit Rapp wrote in the late '30s, combined with material from the "moving into the new apartment" Bickersons sketch. The entire half-hour script is published in the first volume of *The Bickersons Scripts*.

In July of 1970 Phil submitted at least one more script—the Christmas episode, which was approved for pre-production by Krantz himself. In August, a storyboard was being produced to show ABC, and talks for the animated series continued through February, 1971. Krantz went to New York with a short, limited-animation demo (now on The Bickersons DVD) to try to interest advertisers, which put a temporary halt to production. The money men wanted changes to the planned work. The project was still hanging on into April, but things began to fall through. Krantz had wanted Filmation to help with production to assure a 1971 fall season, but they were not

willing to make concessions to the deal Krantz needed. He had spent close to $100,000 to get The Bickersons cartoon picked up, but could not find a home for it. Screen Gems was interested in distributing it, but Rapp's option was quickly running out and Phil was undecided if this was all worth it. Krantz optimistically wrote, "I must tell you that when I was at Screen Gems, we had such difficulty with *Dennis the Menace*, which extended over a period of years, before we finally got the thing off the ground. Other shows have had similar hang-ups." He was certain an extension on the option would help find a home for the series between January and September, 1972.

Rapp possibly did not renew the option since, according to a September 17, 1971 article in *Variety*, Filmation was set to develop the show, though Krantz may have finally found them receptive to a deal. Norm Prescott and Lou Scheimer were to produce The Bickersons with Hal Sutherland set to direct. The budget was set at $60,000-$70,000 per show, with a projected September, 1972 target for primetime showing. Obviously, a nighttime, family audience made more sense than Saturday morning, since, like *The Flintstones*, the protagonists were not dogs and aliens. Sponsor Procter & Gamble, at first very hesitant about laying money on such bittersweet characters, came on board, but only briefly.

For this last effort, to coincide with the submitted new pilot script, Phil Rapp wrote a selection of "Future Projections" (also published, as an Introduction, in *The Bickersons Scripts*), to give animators an idea for possible scripts later on. Some were ambitious, original plots Rapp had never laid down before (John escaping from the snore hospital, chased by cops), mixed with old favorites, and even a capsule version of *Match Please, Darling*.

Naturally, for cartoon reasons, Nature Boy was given a larger, more important role. As Rapp wrote, he was "the Bickerson cat who only thinks of himself as a man but has quite a few of the credentials. Spoiled rotten by the doting affection of Blanche Bickerson, displaying his feline cunning in involving his arch enemy John in hopeless predicaments, Nature Boy is not only one side of the Oedipus triangle but its very apex." One episode, "The Melancholy Dane," put Nature Boy up against a Great Dane which John brings home in self-defense.

Alas, The Bickersons animated series could not defend itself against a lack of interest, rising costs and the fierce competition of the limited-animation jungle.

The Final Years and Beyond

The last few years of original Bickersons material and performances consisted mainly of more radio spots, especially a proficient amount for that creamy, low-cal creation, Coffee Rich. The Bickersons were hired in February of 1975 for a series of eight sixty-second transcribed radio commercials featuring Don Ameche and Frances Langford for Rich Products Corporation, makers of Coffee Rich. Phil was paid $18,000 plus the actual cost of production, and AFTRA pension payments were made on behalf of the two stars. Rich Products also took care of the transportation costs for the stars, including a round-trip flight for Don from Rome to Los Angeles. The contract allowed the commercials to be used for 13 consecutive weeks in 1975, plus the option to replay them the next year for 13 weeks for the sum of $1,500, out of which Rapp paid the stars' royalties.

Below is one unproduced, rather lengthy (and sometimes visually-oriented) first draft spot:

ANNOUNCER: Ladies and gentlemen, here are the celebrated Battling Bickersons as they looked twenty years ago on their first wedding anniversary.

JOHN (O.S.): Blanche, darling!

BLANCHE: Yes, dear?

JOHN: (Enters and kisses her) Happy anniversary.

BLANCHE: John! You remembered!

JOHN: I'll never forget. What's for breakfast?

BLANCHE: There it is, love. (Points to bowl) Right there.

JOHN: (Stares) What is it?

BLANCHE: (Hurt) Oh, John. You know I can only make two things for breakfast. Pig's knuckles or mush.

JOHN: (Still staring into bowl) Uh-huh. Well, which one is this?

BLANCHE: Is that supposed to be funny?

JOHN: No, dear—just a civil question.

BLANCHE: (In tears) You hate my cooking.

JOHN: Oh, sweetheart, I don't hate your cooking. I just don't understand it, that's all. Like that rhubarb pie you made last night. Who ever heard of a pie two feet long?

BLANCHE: Well, I couldn't get any shorter rhubarb.

JOHN: Blanche, will you please buy a cookbook?

BLANCHE: (In tears again) I knew it. You *do* hate my cooking!

JOHN: That's not true. I eat everything you make for me!

BLANCHE: Then why do you always get ptomaine poisoning?

JOHN: Blanche, can I just have some coffee? I'm late for work.

BLANCHE: Not until you try a little of this. (Pushes bowl to him and pours Coffee Rich into it) Eat it.

JOHN: Hey—easy on the cream, Blanche. You know how much that stuff costs, and besides, I'm trying to keep my weight down.

BLANCHE: It isn't cream, silly. It's better than cream and a lot cheaper. This is the new Coffee Rich. It's the leading liquid non-dairy creamer.

JOHN: Coffee Rich?

BLANCHE: And it stays fresh in the refrigerator for three weeks! Please eat your breakfast, John!

JOHN: (Starts to eat) Hey, this is marvelous!

BLANCHE: I'm so happy you like it, John. (Pours on more Coffee Rich) You can use this Coffee Rich on

	anything. Cereal, fruit—anything. And it's got twenty-two less calories per ounce than cream. Finish it, darling.
JOHN:	(Gobbles up food) I won't leave a speck. Blanche, darling—I don't know who gets the credit—you or Coffee Rich—but this is the best mush you ever made in your life!
BLANCHE:	(Starts to sob again)

ABBOTT LABORATORIES
PREAM
ONE 60-SECOND ET RADIO COMMERCIAL
"BIG SAM"
#1-60

(SNORING SOUNDS. BIRDS CHIRPING IN BKGD.)

BLANCHE: John Bickerson! Will you put that fishing pole down long enough to taste this coffee I made for you?

JOHN: Uh. Uh. Where izze? Whereizze?

BLANCHE: Where's who?

JOHN: Big Sam. I've been tryin' to hook that fish for eight years and this year I'm gonna do it.

BLANCHE: In your sleep?

JOHN: I wasn't asleep, Blanche. Don't ya recognize a fish call when you hear one? I was luring Big Sam.

BLANCHE: Well forget about that fish for a minute and taste this coffee. It's got a surprise in it.

JOHN: Bourbon?

BLANCHE: No, Pream. I packed it for the trip. And wait'll you taste it. New Pream tastes even better than cream.

JOHN: Okay, Blanche. Hand me the coffee and I'll --

(SUDDEN WHIRRING OF REEL, WATER SPLASHING.)

Blanche! It's Big Sam! I've hooked Big Sam! (MORE SPLASHING, WHIRRING.) Watch out! Hang on, Big Sam! Oh, no! He got away -- I've lost him!

BLANCHE: Oh, darn! You spilled the coffee, John. Now you won't get to taste new Pream.

JOHN: Pream! Pream! (SOBBING.) What about Big Sam!!!

```
ABBOTT LABORATORIES
PREAM                                       PAGE TWO
ONE 60-SECOND ET RADIO COMMERCIAL
"BIG SAM"
#1-60


BLANCHE:      Well he can't go far, John.  After all, he is in the lake.
              All you have to do is catch him.
JOHN:         (PITIFUL GROAN)
ANNCR:        Try new Pream.  It really does taste better than cream.












RM:bl
8/9/66
REVISED
8/18/66
REVISED
8/24/66
APPROVED
9/6/66
```

```
ABBOTT LABORATORIES
PREAM
ONE 60-SECOND ET RADIO COMMERCIAL
"BREAKFAST TABLE"
#2-60
```

                (TINKLE OF CUP & SAUCER. RATTLE OF NEWSPAPER)

BLANCHE: Jo-ohn ...?

JOHN: Umph.

BLANCHE: John?

JOHN: Umph.

BLANCHE: John Bickerson, will you get your head out of that newspaper! Every morning it's the same! You never pay any attention to me!

JOHN: Mph.

BLANCHE: (SWEETLY) John, guess what I put in your coffee this morning?

JOHN: Mph.

BLANCHE: Catsup!

JOHN: Mph. (PAUSE) What did you say, Blanche?

BLANCHE: I said I put catsup in your coffee.

JOHN: Blanche, you know I like my coffee black.

BLANCHE: Actually, I put some Pream in your coffee. And it's delicious. It actually improves the taste.

JOHN: Blanche, nothing can improve the taste of your coffee.

BLANCHE: Well this does. New Pream tastes even better than cream.

JOHN: Okay, okay -- I'll try it, just for you.

                (PAUSE. SLURPING SOUNDS)

BLANCHE: Well?

JOHN: (SLURP) Tastes just like always. Sweet and sticky.

```
ABBOTT LABORATORIES
PREAM
ONE 60-SECOND ET RADIO COMMERCIAL        PAGE TWO
"BREAKFAST TABLE"
#2-60
```

BLANCHE: That's not the coffee! That's the pancake syrup!
JOHN: Well can I help it if you --
BLANCHE: You never appreciate me! You never pay any --
JOHN: (FADING OUT)   Blanche, I don't even <u>like</u> breakfast --
ANNCR: Try new Pream. It really does taste better than cream.

RM:gt
APPROVED
9/6/66

```
ABBOTT LABORATORIES
PREAM
ONE 60-SECOND ET RADIO COMMERCIAL
"FIVE O'CLOCK"
#3-60
```

        (SNORING SOUNDS.)

        (MORE SNORING SOUNDS)

BLANCHE: John ... Wake up, John.

JOHN: Uh! Uh-uh! Whatsamatter! Whatsamatter!

BLANCHE: I want you to taste this coffee, John.

JOHN: Coffee? Coffee! Blanche, it's five o'clock in the morning! I don't need coffee; I need sleep!

BLANCHE: I couln't help it, John. I've made a discovery and I'm so excited about it, I couldn't wait. I had to share it with you.

JOHN: Blanche -- I share your bed. I share your cooking. I even share your mother! Do I haveta share your discoveries, too? (RESIGNED) Okay, what is it?

BLANCHE: It's new Pream, John. I ran out of cream so I used this Pream in the coffee instead. And it's delicious. Here, taste it.

JOHN: Pream, cream, schmeem. It's five o'clock in the morning, Blanche!

BLANCHE: Taste it, John. New Pream tastes even better than cream!

JOHN: Okay, gimme the coffee.

        (PAUSE. SLURPING SOUNDS.)

BLANCHE: Well?

JOHN: I can't taste a thing. The coffee's cold.

BLANCHE: Cold? Well if you wouldn't take so long --

```
PREAM
ABBOTT LABORATORIES                          PAGE TWO
ONE 60-SECOND ET RADIO COMMERCIAL
"FIVE O'CLOCK"
#3-60


JOHN:       Blanche, all I said was --
BLANCHE:    You never appreciate me!  You never --
JOHN:       Blanche, it's five o'clock in the morning -- (FADE UNDER
            ANNCR.)
ANNCR:      Try new Pream in your coffee.  It really does taste better
            than cream.




                    RM:gt
                    APPROVED
                    9/6/66
```

JOHN: (Bewildered) What's the matter?

BLANCHE: That was pig's knuckles!

As John shakes his head in amazement: FADE OUT

Another commercial in the same series:

JOHN: (SOUND OF SLURPING AND BURBLING)

BLANCHE: John, wake up! You sound like you're snoring under water.

JOHN: Is that illegal?

BLANCHE: You might drown in your sleep.

JOHN: Well, I'm not snoring, I'm drinking coffee.

BLANCHE: At this hour?

JOHN: Your coffee was so good, I dreamed about it. Had to go downstairs and get another cup.

BLANCHE: Why, John, that's the first nice thing you ever said about my cooking.

JOHN: I didn't say you *did* it, Blanche. Maybe the new Coffee Rich you're using did.

BLANCHE: I don't mind sharing the credit with Coffee Rich. After all, you like your coffee strong, and Coffee Rich does smooth away the bitterness.

JOHN: In that case, have a sip. See how good it is.

BLANCHE: John Bickerson—what made you so sweet all of a sudden?

JOHN: Didn't you say Coffee Rich smooths away the bitterness?

BLANCHE: Yes, and I discovered it all by myself. Don't you think that deserves a kiss?

JOHN: A million kisses!

BLANCHE: I mean me—not that carton of Coffee Rich!

JOHN: You're next, Blanche. (KISS)

BLANCHE: John, you kissed me! Let me tell you more good things about Coffee Rich. It's marvelous on fruits and cereals too. (SOUND OF SIPPING COFFEE)

It stays fresh three weeks in the refrigerator. (SOUND OF SIPPING COFFEE) It costs less than cream. And it has fewer calories per ounce.

JOHN: Hey, I said a *sip*—don't drink it all.

BLANCHE: All right, John. When you're as sweet as this I'll do anything for you.

JOHN: Then get up and get me some more coffee.

ANNCR: You just heard Don Ameche and Frances Langford as "The Bickersons." But did you ever hear them sound so loving? Maybe you ought to bring Coffee Rich, the new liquid non-dairy creamer, into *your* marriage. You'll find it at your grocer's freezer in the blue and white carton.

Coffee Rich was assuredly the most prolific sponsor The Bickersons ever had, and the one for which they are still most remembered. The "found" money was glorious for Rapp and so was the freedom he encountered for a last fling on new Bix situations. Aside from the many scripts he (and only he) wrote for the team, even more 60-second spots were plotted:

1. John is complaining about bills at the breakfast table. Blanche spends too much money—just bought a new carpet sweeper because the one she inherited from her mother wore out. "Here, have a cup of coffee, John, with Coffee Rich. Coffee Rich takes the bitterness out of coffee, maybe it will take it out of you."
1a. In a previous version, Blanche makes her Coffee Rich pitch as part of the speech she's going to give to her Club, which is having a contest Friday night for the best speech on economy. The prize is $200.
2. John has a headache and balances the frozen Coffee Rich on his head because it feels good.
2a. In a previous version, John couldn't find the ice bag so balances Coffee Rich on his head. It's thawed now, so Blanche suggests he use it on his breakfast, which is either mush or pig's knuckles.
3. John is putting a padlock on the refrigerator because someone's been getting at his Coffee Rich. Blanche has been feeding it to Nature Boy because it keeps his coat shinny.
4. Blanche complains that she always has to pick up John's things. "What do you think I am—a vacuum cleaner?" "No, Blanche—a vacuum cleaner can be turned off!" He goes to eat his green cereal, with plenty of Coffee Rich to "keep the calories down."
5. John and Blanche are camping in the woods. John was lost in the brush, but comes back to the tent for a steaming cup of coffee with Coffee Rich. She keeps it fresh in the cooler. John didn't catch any trout, but tries to pass off a can of sardines as his catch.

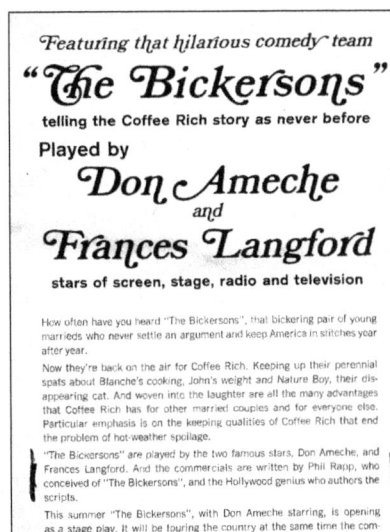

6. John complains about the good coffee at the breakfast table. It's usually bitter, but today it's full of Coffee Rich.
7. John is stuck in a snowdrift. A St. Bernard with Coffee Rich under his neck at last finds him. Blanche skis away for help— and to bring "back some nice hot cereal. Coffee Rich brings out the taste of cereal," she says as she swooshes away.
8. John is awakened from dreadful snoring, but when he turns over on his side, the frozen Coffee Rich wakes him up. Blanche put it in his bed; she wants to thaw it out. It's for his breakfast, but she forgot to take it out in time to thaw.
9. John is duck hunting, but Blanche scares away a whole flock of mallards by bringing him a thermos of coffee, cereal, fruit and two cartons of Coffee Rich to put on everything. He suggests she not stand in front of his shotgun. "I could never prove it was an accident."
10. Blanche has already collected up two shopping carts full of groceries which poor John has to pull and push. And they haven't even yet picked up the Coffee Rich they came in for.

Most commercials had a different slant to accent the diversified features of the product: taste, calories, affordability, economy, ease of use, etc. Sometimes the scripts were for "John and Blanche," sometimes the names written in were "Don and Lang."

At some point in the mid-1970s The Bickersons commercials stopped. Whether it was lack of interest in the sponsor's or on the stars' parts is unknown. Phil Rapp would have preferred an indefinite life to the characters, but he was just about to get that anyway.

At the end of 1975 The Bickersons records were still bringing in money. Catalog # G30523, called sometimes "Breakfast with John and Blanche," and sometimes simply "The Bickersons," was the biggest seller. *The Bickersons* #CD08492 was also bringing in its fifteen cents per record, netting Rapp $189.75 for this royalty statement. So as of 1975, Bix albums were still selling at least over 1,000 copies a year (this statement equaling 1,265 copies). The nostalgia market was blossoming. "Old" never went out of fashion; it was a part of history.

The royalties on the albums were to diminish quite a bit during the next few years, but not before Rapp found himself in talks with Metacom, a company specializing in bringing old-time radio shows back to life through an extensive catalog and amazing distribution through bookstores and retail markets.

In 1978, Metacom offered a deal to Paul Rapp through his attorney Gordon Levoy to carry Bickersons recordings. They guaranteed a minimum royalty over a five-year period plus a monthly accounting. At first Metacom was under the impression that the original Bickersons recordings were no longer under copyright, but as Phil had been involved with producing the CBS records, and part of those recordings were what Metacom had, the company wanted to strike a deal to benefit everyone.

Metacom had been carrying Bickersons recordings already, but Paul Rapp, on Phil's behalf, had informed the FBI that Phil Rapp was the creator and owner of The Bickersons. Metacom claimed that no federal copyright protection existed for sound recordings made prior to February 15, 1972, that they were free and clear to use.

Levoy's letter to Metacom's attorney George H. Frisch asserted that they were correct about the 1972 copyright law, but reminded them of the "literally hundreds of legal decisions affording protection and substantial recovery. There are also many different approaches which have been successfully asserted and accepted by the courts." Including: protection under state common law copyright which has existed since 1834; basic rights by virtue of plagiarism; the principle of unfair competition. Appended to the letter were previous examples of cases involving these: Waring vs. WDAS Broadcasting Station, Metropolitan Opera Co. vs. Wagner Nichols, Stamps vs. Mills Music Inc., Hemingway vs. Film Alliance, and others.

Levoy also reminded them that the name "Bickersons," though not copyrighted, had a secondary meaning which needed to be authorized. "To anyone in the active portion of the entertainment industry, and to the general viewing and listening audiences, the title 'Bickersons' is firmly entrenched and specifically identified with the name of Phil Rapp and his works."

The letter, while not written to offend and was open to a licensing discussion, was in effect a cease and desist letter.

Director of Marketing James I. McCann explained in a September 22, 1978 letter that if the Rapps could furnish proof of their rights, Metacom would like to discuss a non-exclusive use of their shows. They preferred to pay via the number of records made rather than on sales, paying a minimum royalty over a five-year period. Levoy's office was concerned about proving rights, but the Rapp files contained more than enough author and rights proof to secure a long-term Metacom contract that renewed yearly.

At the same time, rumors stated that a pilot of The Bickersons was being shot in Canada with negotiations under way with NBC for a television series starring Steve Lawrence and Edie Gorme. Nothing came of it.

Audio was The Bickersons' lifeblood. In August of 1978, Ann E. Gregory-Bjorklund of Wisconsin got in touch with Rapp about editing three 10-minute Bickersons sketches (Business Trip, Blanche Gets a Dog, and Bets on Horses) into one 10-minute sketch to be performed and directed by Ann and her husband Bob. They would be giving 17 performances between October 8 and 26, fifteen of which would be afternoon luncheon theatre performances for a group of 230+ senior citizen groups from within a 100+ radius of Neenah, Wisconsin. The remaining two evening performances would be comprised of 200+ people aged 40 and above. Ticket prices were $16.50, with each performance being 100 minutes long (50 minutes of singing, 50 minutes of old radio scripts) with a 20-minute intermission. The Happy Days Luncheon Theater paid a troop called The Cat's Pajamas a total of $435 per performance, which included all fees. The program for the performances stated the synopsis: "The action takes place in station WHDT's radio studio, and involves one evening of radio programming." The other shows shown were *Fibber McGee and Molly* by Don Quinn and Phil Leslie, and *The Curly Campbell Show* by Bob Bjorklund.

A perk of the deal for the Rapps was that Ann was able to sell Bickersons cassettes after the shows. Paul sent 150 tapes out to the Gregory-Bjorklund's new home in Excelsior, Minnesota which were then sold for $6.98 each.

Vince Viverito and Ruth Landis also wrote a play, dealing with the off-mike relationship of the characters who play John and Blanche Bickerson on-mike. With permission, they used 5 to 7 minutes worth of material from *The Bickersons Rematch*. The playwrights also hoped to keep film rights open, just in case…The play had been greenlighted by a "major Chicago commercial theatrical producer" to be done at the Apollo Theater Center. It was a situation that would happen several times during the latter years of The Bickersons' fan base.

On July 28, 1980, a contract was signed between Phil and Radio Renaissance to create a new Bickersons radio pilot show based upon the old scripts and characters, to be produced in Canada and globally distributed. Phil received $1,500 (Canadian dollars) for exclusive option to The Bickersons name in Canada for 180 days and world radio broadcast rights to all Bickersons material. $250 (Canadian) would be paid for each and every sketch produced in preparation for the coming series, plus 10% of the net receipts.

That November *The Toronto Star* proclaimed "The battling Bickersons are back at it," in a report from Bruce Blackadar. Rapp was in Toronto that week to direct the six new segments, produced by Bob Jarvis and Sandra O'Neill. Bill Walker and Sylvia Lennick were signed on as the new John and Blanche.

Jarvis: "We think the comedy in the series is timeless. It's the battle of the sexes, and that never changes. It's the old three o'clock in the morning thing and his snoring wakes her up and they fight…I remember it still from when it was on the radio in the '40s and '50s.

"And Phil just blows me away. He was a contemporary of George Burns, in vaudeville…In the Depression he wrote and produced two Broadway plays in one year, he was making about $20,000 a week. He's done everything.

"We had a hard time tracking him down. I'd been after him for these rights for 15 years." Jarvis hoped to sell the series by the beginning of '81. Whether or not new material was recorded is open to question.

As of April 1981, there was still interest in a Bickersons animation series. Paul Rapp gave Ross LaManna permission to submit a proposal to

Hanna-Barbera to produce an animated or live-action Bickersons series, but again nothing happened.

The name still had pulling power, though. United Airlines had programmed a Bickersons album into their in-flight entertainment in November of 1981 "because we feel it is an excellent piece of humor that cuts across all age groups." Over 4 million passengers had an opportunity to hear the comedy in the two months it was broadcast.

During all this time talks were still going strong with Metacom for a final and official release. New titles for January 1984 had to be finalized by June 1, 1983. The royalty rate was on a "second-level" scale for properties, paying out royalties of 10 cents per show which Metacom believed would add up to $5,000 at least for The Bickersons per year. Paul Rapp told them that The Bickersons was already optioned in full, but he would be glad to discuss the situation with them when the contract was up.

Paul had informed his attorney Levoy of Metacom's eagerness on March 22, 1983, but rights were still exclusively held by a radio station (WJOK in Gaithersburg, MD 1150 AM) that played comedy 24 hours a day. The Bickersons was their #1 most requested recording, and the royalties from those plays (and the direct sales they provoked) exceeded Metacom's offer. That financial fact, plus the exclusivity that Metacom wanted, caused Paul not to accept their offer without a revised agreement. The Bickersons had been optioned in six-month increments for the last two years, recently extended for six more months.

The Rapps were seeing a lot of direct sales from cassettes they were producing. In 1983-4, WJOK, as part of their agreement, was promoting the sale of Bickersons cassettes over the air. They weren't set up to process orders, but they passed out information. Their broadcast copy energetically solicited a lot of interest:

"The Bickersons are back at last!! For nearly two years now, the quarreling and bickering John and Blanche Bickerson have been the most requested routines on WJOK. Hundreds of our listeners have been asking how they can get copies of those great old radio shows starring Don Ameche and Frances Langford. Well, they're finally available. WJOK has been in touch with the creator of the programs, Philip Rapp, and we're pleased to announce that several of the most popular shows are now available on cassette. Listen…remember this?? (Plays short Bickerson routine). You won't find this material in any store. But if you want it for your library, just send us your name and address on a postcard and we'll forward you the information on how to order it. Send your name and address today to WJOK, 20201 Watkins Mill Rd., Gaithersburg, MD 20879."

The Rapps also began putting out Bickersons recordings in 1984 through a company in Excelsior, Minnesota. Ads were placed in major magazines such as *World Press Review, The New Republic, The Atlantic* and others. Sales were healthy.

No wonder James I. McCann, president of Metacom, wanted those exclusive rights plus the rights for immediate radio airplay. Otherwise, he didn't want to discuss the deal further. Licensing and packaging had to occur without delay so that tapes could be out for Christmas 1983. It would cost them $10,000 that year just preparing the artwork and the packaging.

Five years previously, Metacom operated under the theory that all radio programs were in public domain so they weren't receptive to licensing requests. But after three lawsuits with estates of radio copyright owners, they paid $250,000 in back royalties and set up licensing. The royalties paid out to licensors in 1982 alone was six figures. During the fiscal year ending September 30, 1983, Metacom manufactured over 2 million old radio shows. They were 25% bigger than their only licensed competitor, Nostalgia Lane.

A year later, ten titles of The Bickersons were part of the Metacom catalog. But there were also pirates sailing the waters of pre-internet nostalgia. On January 1, 1987 Paul Rapp wrote to Metacom: "I have had a chance to peruse the Xerox copy of a record album entitled "The Return of the Bickersons!" and to listen to the tapes. First, let me say that I have never heard of these pirates and I can assure you they will wish they never heard from me. That aside, I will make some points. They are clearly guilty of a number of serious crimes. Copyright violation, unfair competition, false advertising, forgery, and libel, to name a few. Such blatant piracy is shocking. Since Metacom now has the license to sell *The Bickersons* as contracted by me it is obvious that you must move swiftly to cause them to cease and desist. Before I take any action I would like a report from you as to what and how you are going to proceed. Metacom is all too familiar with how I deal with people who steal my father's property. I have records of payment for royalties dating back to 1960 to the very present and since these thieves claim to have been marketing the property since 1970 to the present, I shall not take the matter lightly. As you know I have been acquiring a number of the old radio shows to add to your catalogue of present material that you now have. I would like to impress upon you that

I am currently talking with networks to put *The Bickersons* on TV and as you well know the option for same is held by MGM."

Metacom was jealous and forceful of their rights, as big businesses are who invest a lot of money in a product. Cease and decease letters were sent on February 10, 1987 to infringing sellers, such as Jonathan Sonneborn, president of Premier Electronic Laboratories Inc. in the case of making and selling Bickersons tapes.

Though Metacom no longer exists, the nostalgia market continues to thrive, as conventions, traders, and sellers (legit and otherwise) keep the OTR world spinning.

Even today, Bickerson mp3 CDs abound in an era of instant downloading and fervent ebay.com bidding.

Official recordings of The Bickersons have never been out of print. They are currently for sale in bookstores, Walmart, etc. by way of Radio Spirits, the largest seller of old-time radio shows, and at bickersons.com listeners can find an extensive catalog of CDs and DVDs. The comedy is indeed timeless, and from time to time talks renew about new series (radio and television). The Rapps met with Fox TV in the early 1980s about a series then, but when Phil failed to give up his rights to the characters in a contract, things fell through. Soon after that meeting, *Married with Children* began an incredible reign that arguably created the 4th TV network.

Thanks to the name "Bickersons," John and Blanche have forever been in the public eye. They define a type that will never go out of style. Book, film and play (*Chess*, for instance) reviews have mentioned The Bickersons through the years. In the Sunday paper—January 29, 1984—there was a *BC* cartoon by Johnny Hart alluding to The Bickersons via Don Ameche. Everyone knew them. Paul Rapp even sent a Bickersons album to Prince Charles and Lady Diana, as a wedding present. The Prince's secretary wrote a cordial reply that stated that Charles was a fan and considered himself and Diana to be The Bickersons.

Joel Rapp: "We used to keep track of all the references to The Bickersons in the print media—we have been taking it for granted for years. Among the literally hundreds of examples which made The Bickersons a virtual part of the language, I recall a reference in *M*A*S*H* in which The Bickersons was mentioned over a loudspeaker; I think it was something about Hot Lips and the doctor she was playing house with."

As long as there's heat and passion and financial straits and a good, strong snore and love, The Bickersons will prevail and live on through us all.

Mary and Phil Rapp.

Philip Rapp

Bickersons instigator Philip Rapp was born on March 26, 1907 in England. His Austrian-born parents brought him to the United States at an early age where he began a dancing act with another fellow, writing and selling gags on the side for sometimes even better money. One of the most gifted comedy writers of his time, he wrote many skits for comics of the early '30s. The money was much easier for him, so he gave up performing for writing. 1932 saw Phil writing for Eddie Cantor's radio show for an impressive salary. He also directed *The Eddie Cantor Show* in 1936-37, while contributing special material to Cantor's film *Strike Me Pink* and Jimmy Durante's *Start Cheering*.

During his stint as screenwriter for Danny Kaye in the 1940s, he penned such hits as *Wonder Man, The Secret Life of Walter Mitty,* and *The Inspector General*. He also worked as a gag man for MGM, having an office there at the time. It was his Golden Age. During those years, he came up with one of the classic radio comedy teams of all time: The Bickersons. He would also be called upon by other comics and directors to punch up already-written radio scripts, or helm the production itself by directing.

During all this time Rapp was also working on Baby Snooks, which he created in 1936. There are differing stories on when and who did create the Snooks character, which Ziegfeld comedienne Fanny Brice made into an eternal radio star. Some references claim that the character was first introduced in a Ziegfeld Follies stage show long before Rapp was involved with the radio series *Ziegfeld Follies of the Air* and *Maxwell House Coffee Time*, while Rapp himself recalls that the aforementioned Follies series was really the start of it. Regardless, the little girl with the chronic "Why?"

launched into her own radio show in 1944 which lasted through 1951, when Fanny died.

Rapp also wrote for the stage. He contributed material for *The Ziegfeld Follies of '33*, wrote *Spring In Brazil* (a musical starring Milton Berle) for the Shuberts, and penned a Bickersons play entitled *Match Please, Darling* with his son Joel. There were other theatrical collaborations, but his main success was in radio and television.

As radio succumbed to the new visual medium, Rapp began slowly adapting his Bickersons for guest shots on many series, and a regular spot on *Star Time*, which he co-wrote and directed. He wrote and directed other early TV series, including: the first variety show for TV, *The Dumont Star Time Revue*, which ran from 1949 to 1951; the pilot of *I Married Joan*, in 1952 for Joan Davis; *Squeegee*, a series for Ben Blue in 1955; and 22 episodes of *The Adventures of Hiram Holliday* for NBC in 1957, which starred Wally Cox as an unlikely adventure hero. *Hiram* was quite popular, but was soon cancelled, as it was up against *The Wonderful World of Disney*.

In the 1950s Rapp had his biggest TV hit with the *Topper* series, based on the best-selling book by Thorne Smith. This lovable show featured Leo G. Carroll as bank vice president Cosmo Topper suffering through the adventures of happy ghosts, John and Marion Kirby, and their ghost-dog Neil. Rapp served as head writer and director. 78 episodes were filmed, running from October 1953 to September 1955. Several of the early shows were written by composer Stephen Sondheim. Reruns were frequent and though hard-to-find now, are still held in reverence today.

The decade ended with a possible new series called *Deputy Seraph*, that was to reunite the three Marx Brothers for television. Alas, it was called off when Chico couldn't be insured, due to atherosclerosis. Rapp had promised Groucho a Rolls-Royce if the pilot sold. Unfortunately, it did not sell, and the Marx Brothers' scenes were the only portions ever filmed.

From 1960 to 1961, Rapp served as Executive Producer for *The Tab Hunter Show*, and continued to write and pitch TV series. In later years, Phil made good money by writing TV and radio commercials featuring the Bickersons, for Coffee Rich, General Motors, and others. Cleverly, Rapp always retained total artistic control, as well as the rights to his creations.

Rapp wrote over 600 scripts for Baby Snooks and The Bickersons alone, the latter being what he considered his legacy. When he died on

January 23, 1996 in Beverly Hills, his *New York Times* obituary began by crediting him as the creator of The Bickersons, with other notices going on at length about the quarrelsome duo. His comedy legacy continues to live on.

Don Ameche

John Bickerson was born Dominic Felix Amici on May 31, 1908, in Kenosha, Wisconsin. The second child of four boys and four girls, he was the son of a saloon-keeping Italian immigrant, with a mother of German and Scotch-Irish descent. Though the family called him Dom, it was soon changed to Don by kids in school who found that more natural to pronounce.

While studying law in college, he chanced to show up at an audition with a friend and, on a lark, got up to audition with the others. The director thought him the best there, and that started the acting bug biting. Ameche quickly gave up law to appear in a few college shows before graduating to make a 1929 debut on Broadway in *Jerry for Short*. He was not an immediate sensation, so he toured with Texas Guinan on the vaudeville circuit, then joined a stock company. His big break came on radio, appearing in several hot Chicago properties such as *The First Nighter*, *The Empire Builder* and romances such as *Betty and Bob*. Constant wireless work soon gained the ear of Hollywood.

In 1935, Darryl F. Zanuck, 20th Century-Fox mogul, tested him for pictures, and Don's long film career had began. He debuted in *Sins of Man* the following year, and found his niche as the dashing young lead in many a drama, comedy and musical. His light baritone voice kept his career more diverse than most actors, allowing him to sing before the Ritz Brothers in *The Three Musketeers* (1939) and other hit films. He sometimes teamed with Alice Faye and Tyrone Power (though not always together) in classics such as *You Can't Have Everything* (1937), *In Old Chicago* (1937), and *Alexander's Ragtime Band* (1938).

The most famous role of his career came in 1939 when he invented the telephone as *Alexander Graham Bell*, and he never lived it down. For

Don Ameche and Mary Martin in *Kiss the Boys Goodbye*.

years after, Ameche was synonymous with the telephone, prompting some wise guy to label said device "the Ameche" for a while. Don had to put up with the jokes (sometimes in his own films) and being stereotyped in a few movies and television shows as an inventor, but it kept him in the public eye, and it kept him working. His work ethic would remain strong and steady throughout his life. He lived to act, sometimes at the cost of spending time with his beloved family (four sons and two daughters).

Ameche's favorite role came in 1943 when Ernst Lubitsch cast him as the repentant lead in *Heaven Can Wait*, a period family comedy in which Ameche tells his life story to the devil, who finally realizes he's come to the wrong place.

His illustrious film career began to wind down when he made the terrible mistake (which he would regret later) of not renewing his contract with Fox, but turning freelance so that he could be in control of the roles he played. Unfortunately, the roles offered him were not Hollywood's best, and he quietly slipped into more radio and television work which was becoming much easier to find.

In 1946 he stepped into the role of John Bickerson on radio in *Drene Time* and never snored out of it. Though Lew Parker took over the role in a 1951 radio series and *Star Time* on television, he came back for two highly successful Columbia albums. But his real comeback into the field of starring entertainment came a few years earlier when he joined the cast of Cole Porter's last stage musical, *Silk Stockings*. He introduced the hit, "All of You," assuring a short but busy Broadway career in several other shows.

In 1961 he became host of the TV series *International Showtime*, which brought European circuses into the homes of America. It lasted four years, allowing Ameche to see the world and sample its fine cuisine and wines. A feature film, with rich narration by Ameche, was released the following year compiling the best lion acts, balancers and clowns from the series.

When the 1970s came around, pickings were lean for Don. He kept busy with mostly regional theatre performances, and the occasional short bit in films (like 1970's *Suppose They Gave a War and Nobody Came?*), and guest starring on high-profile TV series (*Quincy, Ellery Queen, Columbo, The Love Boat*), but again, his parts were short and seemed to want his name more than his performances.

It was as one of the scheming financial villains in *Trading Places* in 1983 that brought Ameche back to the limelight, to huge acclaim. The Duke brothers (Ameche and Ralph Bellamy) make a bet that they can turn anyone into a success by just giving him the means to make it happen. Poor Dan Ackroyd switches places with Eddie Murphy, creating one of the biggest comedy hits of the '80s. It turned Don Ameche's life around. He was not only not without work for his remaining years, but, at last, he consistently saw his name above the title once again.

In 1985 he won the Oscar for the rejuvenated pensioner Art Selwyn who, along with other old cronies in Florida, finds the fountain of youth via aliens with strange healing powers. *Cocoon* was a sleeper hit that spawned a less-than-stellar hit sequel three years later, with the original cast reprising their roles.

With the Academy Award firmly and gratefully in hand, Ameche spent his remaining years working hard. Often the roles were restricted to supporting work, but sometimes he shared a lot of screen time, such as opposite Tom Selleck in *Folks* (1992), and as the voice of poor old Shadow, the elder dog in *Homeward Bound: The Incredible Journey* (1993). After filming *Corrina, Corrina* (released the year after his death), Don Ameche died of prostrate cancer on December 6, 1993.

Frances Langford

Blanche Bickerson was born Frances Newbern Langford on April 4, 1914 in Lakeland, Florida. The daughter of concert pianist Annie Newbern, she naturally attended Southern College in Florida to study music. Her plans for a career in opera were snipped short after a tonsillectomy at age 17 modified her high soprano into a contralto, perfect for the husky, sexy sound she was to be known for.

Now setting her vocal sights on popular music, she quickly gained the attention of Tampa's Eli Witt, cigar manufacturer and millionaire, who had heard her perform at an American Legion party. She was paid $5 a week to croon on his local radio show, and soon gained the eye of singer Rudy Vallee, always seeking fresh voices to bring to national radio. Auditioning for Vallee, she sang only 16 bars when he said, "That's enough." He immediately invited her to be his guest star on his radio show the following week in New Orleans. When he invited her to perform in New York, she was able to sing at Cole Porter's birthday party where Hollywood producers were in attendance, including Walter Wanger of Paramount, who was so taken with her performance, he gave her a contract without a screen test.

She made a few unreleased Victor Records in 1931, then recorded for Columbia, made two musical shorts for Warner Brothers' Vitaphone series, and had a bit in the short-lived Peter Arno Broadway musical, *Here Goes the Bride* in 1931.

For most of 1933 Frances sang at the Petit Palais in Manhattan. "There was no real show," she said. "I just got up and sang."

Radio work was constant. From January 7 to February 11, 1934 she sang on NBC's *The Spartan Hour* with Richard Himber's popular band; and from June to November of that year she was routinely heard on *The Joe Cook Show*. From 1934 to 1938 she was the reigning vocalist on *Hollywood Hotel*, a musical variety show, and the first major network series to

Frances Langford is *The Bamboo Blonde*.

broadcast from the West Coast. Hosted by Louella Parsons, the 60-minute show had a glamorous *Grand Hotel* feel to it, as everyone from regular Dick Powell to Carole Lombard found themselves in its lobby.

Back at Paramount, in 1935 she was off to Hollywood for her acting debut in *Every Night at Eight* with Alice Faye and Patsy Kelly. It was her big break, introducing the song "I'm in the Mood for Love," which became her signature tune.

A string of films and a Decca Records deal followed: *Broadway Melody of 1936* (1935), *Collegiate* (1936), Cole Porter's *Born to Dance* (1936) with Eleanor Powell, and Warner Brothers' *Hollywood Hotel* (1937), inspired by the radio show. Her song hits included "I've Got You Under My Skin" (possibly her second most popular song), "Easy to Love," and "I Don't Want to Make History."

Taking some time off to marry actor Jon Hall (most famous for *The Hurricane* in 1937) on June 4, 1938, Frances soon returned to Decca, backed by the likes of Victor Young and Jimmy Dorsey. She made several films in 1940: *Dreaming Out Loud* (with radio's Lum and Abner), *Too Many Girls* (starring Lucille Ball), *The Hit Parade of 1941*. The next year she dyed her beautiful brunette hair to blonde for *All-American Co-Ed*, remaining that way for the rest of her career. She meanwhile continued her prodigious radio work, such as singing on *The Texaco Star Theater* in 1939.

Her first overseas trip with Bob Hope was to Alaska. Enjoying it so much, she stayed with him for years. She also appeared as a regular on his radio show for many years after 1939. She was part of his first military program (at March Field near Pasadena, California) in 1941, kicking off a tour of American training bases. She was eager to do something for her country and gave the boys of the second World War a sweet velvet voice to match her lovely pin-ups.

Somehow, she found time to make more films, including the glorious, Oscar-winning *Yankee Doodle Dandy* (1942), the story of George M. Cohan, for which James Cagney won the Academy Award in the lead role. Irving Berlin wrote a new song, "What Does He Look Like?" for her to sing in the film version of his hit stage show, *This Is the Army* (1943).

Later that year she was given a day's notice to hop a bomber headed for Alaska to join Bob Hope on his touring USO show, which played 36 Army camps there before rounding out a hundred on that one tour. She found the pace exhilarating. They performed three to five shows a week, in addition to the weekly radio show. Bob, Frances, announcer Bill Goodwin, bug-eyed Jerry Colonna and bandleader Skinnay Ennis pulled out all the stops, quickly finding out that it was much easier to make servicemen laugh than studio audiences. The troupe sailed to Europe and the South Pacific, performing in nearly every camp and hospital that had a US soldier in it. It brought comedy, class and song to an otherwise starved and homeless group of American solders; it brought Hope more honors than any single entertainer on earth; and it brought Frances Langford a whirl of harrowing and tender memories that she keeps to this day.

In 1944 Hope was asked by a Special Service marine officer to bring his act to a little island called Pavuvu where the First Marine Division was training for the invasion of Peleliu. They hadn't had any entertainment for nine months. Frances Langford, Jerry Colonna, dancer Patty Thomas, and Bill Goodwin had never turned down a request to do a show, and they didn't this time. The trouble was, there was no landing field on Pavuvu, so the troupe had to go in Cubs (small planes), one person per pilot, landing on a road. The 15,000 men looked up at the sky, and cheered each Cub as it took off after the show. The spectacle of all those marines, some of whom wouldn't be coming back, cheering, meant a lot to Bob.

During some of her tours, she kept a journal which she turned into a newspaper column. The laughs and the struggles were dealt with realistically, but light-hearted enough to interest many readers, resulting in a *lot* more fan mail. She also told it like it was: "I sang to boys, without arms or legs, boys in wheelchairs and on stretchers, and boys in casts from their heads down to their feet.

"When I walked into the first ward and saw all those boys gathered there I got a lump in my throat as big as an egg. I didn't think I would be able to sing or talk. But as I stood there for a second and looked at them, I knew what they wanted. And that's what they were going to get.

"When I finished singing, I noticed a nurse coming towards me leading a soldier carrying a bunch of roses. He presented them to me and said they were just a token of appreciation, not only from the boys there but for all the wounded boys I had ever sung for.

"I can't explain the feeling I had in my heart at that moment.

"The soldier was not more than 18 years old. He was blind in both eyes and his right eye was gone.

"It's things like that that make one feel no matter how much we are doing, it's still too little."

Frances was honored at the Women in War and Victory pageant given at the Chicago Stadium on a Sunday evening in 1945. She had only just returned that July from another long-distance tour with Bob Hope, and was just setting down to make a long-overdue return to the silver screen by way of RKO when the Victory gala called. She interrupted the production of the film, knowing how important it was to honor the women who served in the war. And naturally, she sang.

World War II kept Frances busy. Aside from her Purple Heart Girl duties, she was heard on a plethora of radio shows such as *Command Performance, The Frank Morgan Show*, and *Southern Cruise* (with Dick Powell). But her film career suffered after the war, and she was cast in low-budget musicals like PRC's *Dixie Jamboree* and RKO's *Radio Stars on Parade*. She obviously didn't need the exposure, with radio doing so much for her.

After an extensive tour of veterans' hospitals throughout the country, Frances returned to radio on *Drene Time* in December 1946 to create The Bickersons. Don Ameche and Frances were sometimes heard on *The Charlie McCarthy Show* as the feuding couple, though Marsha Hunt's Blanche 1948 episodes are easier to locate.

Frances and her husband, Jon Hall, appeared in only one film together: *Deputy Marshal* from 1949, in which Frances sang two songs, and Hall's film career by this point was winding down.

When television, with its wobbly cardboard sets and nerve-racking live broadcasting, began to replace radio, Frances Langford was there to give it a touch of grace. From 1950 to 1952 she could seen on *Star Time* (with Don Ameche), *Cavalcade of Stars, The Jack Carter Show, The Ed Wynn Show, Star of the Family, Paul Whiteman's Goodyear Revue, The Ken Murray Show, The Alan Young Show, The Colgate Comedy Hour* and others. Meantime, she sang one number in what turned out to be her last film appearance, *The Glenn Miller Story*, in a WWII scene of entertaining the troops overseas.

In August of 1955 Frances and Jon divorced. On October 6, 1955 she married Ralph Evinrude, owner of Evinrude motorboats, whom she'd met while playing a nightclub in Milwaukee, Wisconsin. They were married aboard his 110-foot yacht, The Chanticleer, and she gave up her film career. But not recording. The next year she recorded "When You Speak with Your Eyes" and "Rocking in the Rocket Room" on the RKO Unique label. Her television career also slowed but did not stop. In the late '50s and early '60s she reappeared on television in *The Frances Langford Special*, *The Bob Hope Special* and a few more, but she was basically retired. In 1967 she returned to NBC for *Perry Como's Kraft Music Hall* and *Hollywood Palace* on ABC.

In the 1960s she did sometimes sing at *The Outrigger*, her Florida club. It was just part of a large complex, including a marina and 40 luxurious motel units. But life on a 300-acre estate with a loving husband was enough for her. Ducks, geese and more than 50 peacocks roamed the land originally built on Kissimmee Swamp, hung together by a spectacular series of footpaths and stylish bridges. Only the Vietnam War gave her reason enough to leave, entertaining more troops with Bob Hope (and sometimes without) in 1966. She continued to work sporadically with Don Ameche in Bickersons commercials and record albums, but most of her time was happily spent at home.

At age 64 she had successful open-heart surgery in March of 1978. When her husband Ralph Evinrude died in 1986, Frances sold her restaurant-marina the two of them built in the 1960s. The new owner dedicated a room to her, complete with her photos, a blown-up radio magazine and celebrity letters written to her.

In later years Frances has been called upon to reminice about her Bob Hope and war years, on specials such as *Entertaining the Troops*, a PBS documentary. But today she is happiest sailing *The Chanticleer* to Mexico, the Bahamas and her delightful Georgian Bay in Canada where she has "little island with a cabin on it. The mountains are all around." She lives on a 57-acre estate overlooking the Indian River in Jensen Beach, Florida, 100 miles north of Miami. Her boat also is stuck together with autographed photos from Presidents and old friends.

She's since remarried, to Harold Stuart, once the assistant secretary of the Air Force under President Harry Truman.

A staunch supporter of her beloved Florida homeland, Frances has given much back to the community. Not only has she Langford Park named after her on Dixie Highway, near the Historic Jensen Beach Arch, but "the Frances Langford Visitor Center welcomes the general public by showcasing marine displays and exhibits designed to fascinate both young and old. Aquariums, touch tanks, educational videos, mounted fish displays, interactive computers and a replica of the Saballariid reef are only some of the highlights found."

Lew Parker

Lewis Parker was born Lewis Austin Jacobs in Brooklyn, NY on October 29, 1910. His mother was Florence Austin and his father was Lewis Jacobs who led a blackface act called Parker and Decker. The duo broke up when Mr. Parker married and "retired into business."

It wasn't long before little Lew felt the theatrical bug biting as well. Though the elder Parker was not enamored of his son choosing such an iffy occupation, after his father died, Lew ventured into his first job: appearing in the chorus of Bobby Clark and Paul McCullough's *The Ramblers* (written by Guy Bolton). Still in high school, he commuted daily from his Brooklyn home to be in the cast, finally giving up school for the part. That venture was almost cut short, however, when he was fired for being late for a number on opening night. Luckily the director changed his mind, giving Lew plenty of chances to season his musical comedy prowess with long New York and Chicago runs. It also gave Lew the huge itch to become a professional comedian.

"When *The Ramblers* went on the road," Parker recalled, "Paul McCullough gave me a few comedy bits of his, because he knew I wanted more than anything else to have my own act." While polishing up what worked, and throwing out what didn't, Parker met comedian Joe Cook in Detroit at a party. Joe thoroughly applauded the act that Lew and another man had worked up together, and he gave them a few jokes to use and told them to write him if they needed any help.

In Cleveland, at another party, Georgie Price was equally encouraging, urging the young team to get into vaudeville. That was all the confidence they needed. Lew and his partner left *The Ramblers* in Chicago and began 20 weeks of bookings in the Midwest.

After the act split up, Lew took a small part in *Girl Crazy* with Willie Howard, who also took an interest in the bright comic; Howard put Parker into his act which played at the Palace. Always touring, Parker found himself playing various vaudeville dates with Milton Berle, learning a lot about technique and timing from The Master. As a solo act, he found himself playing at a lot of Loew's State theatres and other vaudeville houses around the circuit: El Rancho Vegas, Chicago's Palmer House, the Roxy, the Paramount and the Palace in New York, among others.

It was his love for comedy, and especially musical comedy, that caused Lew to search out more versatile roles, like Vincent Youmans' tuneful *Rainbow*. After that, parts in other musicals followed, such as Rodgers and Hart's *Spring Is Here* (1929), *Heads Up!* (1929) with Victor Moore and Ray Bolger, and *Girl Crazy* (1930) with Ethel Merman, Willie Howard and Ginger Rogers. Later that decade, he found his biggest show yet—Cole Porter's *Red Hot and Blue!* (1936), starring Jimmy Durante, Ethel Merman and Bob Hope.

It was appearing in the revue *Ballyhoo of 1932*, with the still relatively unknown Bob Hope, that proved to be the turning point in Parker's career. When Hope's stooge fell ill for a performance, Parker substituted. This began a friendship and mutual admiration which later led Hope to offer Parker his standard act to use, when Hope had been signed for the musical *Roberta* in 1933. Lew Parker used that act for a year.

"I've always been interested in the comics of every show I've been in," Parker remarked, "and for some strange reason the comics were always interested in helping me."

In 1941 Parker began an almost two-year run for the United Service Organizations in the South and Southwest Pacific. Jack Benny had caught one of his G.I. shows, and enthusiastically recommended Lew to Richard Kollmar and James W. Gardiner, the producers of yet another musical, *Are You With It?*, written by songwriter Harry Revel and Arnold B. Horwitt. He appeared as the carnival barker, Goldie, later reprising the role for the movie version in 1948. The musical play starred June Richmond, Dolores Gray and Joan Roberts.

Later, he took over the Ole Olsen role in Olsen and Johnson's hot musical *Hellzapoppin'* when it toured. He also appeared in the plays *The Front Page*, *Inside USA*, Moliere's *The Amorous Flea*, and *George White's Scandals*.

In the late 1940s, television was rearing its ugly head, and new talent was needed. And a lot of it. One of the current hits was a show called *Star Time*, with Frances Langford.

Though Don Ameche regularly appeared as John Bickerson, even on television, when he wasn't available (due to his many films or other committments), Lew Parker was given the difficult task of replacing the master snorer. "Part of the reason he was cast," explains Paul Rapp, "was because he just always looked tired."

While *Star Time* was in rehearsals, Philip Rapp commented, "Lew's earnest, sincere and has genuine quality. I always knew him to be a funny man, but after watching him in a few rehearsals of the Bickersons, I am convinced that he is an infinitely better actor than a comedian."

Star Time went out over the Dumont network, with the Benny Goodman Sextet providing the rollicking music. When the series ended on February 27, 1951, Lew began a short stint as co-host, giving away merchandise on the daytime giveaway show, *Your Surprise Store*. It lasted from May 12 to June 27, 1952. He also appeared on Ed Sullivan's *Toast of the Town*, *The Philip Morris Show*, *Texaco Star Theatre*, *All Star Revue*, *This Is Show Business* and *Cavalcade of Stars* in the 1950s.

On Monday, April 18, 1955 Lew appeared in the musical comedy *Ankles Aweigh* with wife Betty Kean and her sister Jane. Book by Guy Bolton and Eddie Davis, music by Sammy Fain with lyrics by Dan Shapiro and staged by Fred F. Finklehoffe, the story concerned the interrupted honeymoon of a Hollywood starlet and her Navy flier in the Mediterranean. Full of tap dancing, old-fashioned chorus songs and a gag-filled script, it ran for 176 performances in the New York's Mark Hellinger Theatre, yet didn't return its investment. Lew's long-time friend Jackie Gleason loved it. "*Ankles Aweigh* is the most remarkable musical I've ever seen ... a wonderful show from start to finish...with wonderful Betty and Jane Kean. I enjoyed every minute of it." Lew was also featured on the Decca original cast recording released that same year.

The next year, Lew played Broadway with Sammy Davis, Jr. in *Mr. Wonderful* at the Broadway Theatre. It told the story of Charlie Welch's (Davis) rise to the top of showbiz, and sported the hit song "Too Close For Comfort."

Later, Lew played nightclubs and some Las Vegas hotels, especially at the Sands where he performed with wife Betty, Frank Sinatra and others. In 1958 he attained one of his few film roles, that of a character named Lew

Parker in *Country Music Holiday,* a musical with June Carter Cash, Zsa Zsa Gabor and Jesse White.

Aside from John Bickerson, Lew's most important and popular role is probably that of ever-faithful Lou Marie, father of Ann, played by Marlo Thomas, on television's *That Girl*. Rosemary DeCamp, who played Marlo's mother and Lou's wife, said that Lew "was a popular part of its format, lovable and funny with his big eyes and sad, comic face."

Harold Gould originally played "Mr. Brewster" (later renamed Lou Marie) in the unaired pilot from 1965. Unfortunately, to network executives and the show's producers Gould seemed "too Jewish" for what the series was going for. (Everyone loved Gould's performance, however, and he was in fact again the father in another pilot for a hit TV series: *Happy Days.*) Through his friendship with Danny Thomas, Lew auditioned for Lou Marie in 1965, got the part, and until 1971 he was the perfect "reactor," shouting like John Bickerson and constantly surprised by his liberated daughter and her boyfriend, played by Ted Bessell. Bessell was one of many actors who found it hard to retain a straight face when it came to playing opposite the Stone Face of television, Mr. Lew Parker.

Lou Marie owned a French restaurant in Brewster, New York called La Parisianne, and on *That Girl* loved three things more than anything else: his optimistic daughter, his stalwart wife, and his artistic cooking ability. Lew portrayed the barking father with much the same conviction and loudness that John Bickerson required. Minus the snoring.

According to co-creator and co-excecutive producer Bill Persky, Lou's character was based on Danny Thomas more than anyone else. Commenting on his first episode with Marlo Thomas, Lew explained, "She took my arm and said, 'We'll take this until you feel comfortable in the part. I'll stay until midnight if necessary.' I think she is a great talent. I find I'm developing a strong, fatherly feeling toward her."

That Girl ran from September 8, 1966 to September 10, 1971 and influenced a generation. Shortly after its end, Lew returned to his theatre roots and appeared in a Broadway revival of Stephen Sondheim's *A Funny Thing Happened on the Way to the Forum*, playing the part of Senex. It opened on March 30, 1972, though Lew did not perform on opening night. Sadly, Lew collapsed on stage and was taken to St. Clare's Hospital where Marlo would bring him ice cream and talk. Lew asked to see "the birthday show" and together they cried and watched "Paper Hats and Everything" from February 9, 1967. It was then that Lew asked Marlo to do his eulogy.

Lew Parker died of cancer on October 27, 1972, the day before his 65th birthday. The service was held at the Universal Funeral Chapel at 2 p.m. on October 29th. A crying Marlo Thomas gave the eulogy.

Marsha Hunt. (*Laura Wagner*)

Marsha Hunt
by Laura Wagner

She was born Marcia Virginia Hunt on October 17, 1917 in Chicago, Illinois, moving with her parents and older sister Marjorie to New York City when she was just a baby. "From the age of three or four, I wanted to be an actress," Marsha told Jimmy Bangley in a 1997 interview in *Classic Images*. "I was never stage struck—only movies ... I always knew I would be an actress. I prepared in my young life for my ambition. When I was about to graduate from high school at age 16, I searched in vain for any college where I could major in drama." Finding no suitable college for such a career move, the determined girl instead was enrolled at Theodora Irvine's Studio for the Theatre.

To also prepare, the already striking-looking Hunt became a Powers Model "to learn visuals, makeup and grooming. I also wanted to learn how I photographed and to possess confidence in front of a camera. This takes discipline."

It was a discipline that paid off in 1935, when she was asked to screen test at Paramount Pictures. She was accepted right away, and in June of '35, the seventeen-year-old newcomer signed with the studio at $250 a week. Although she asserted that "I wanted to act. Do character roles," Paramount, starting with *The Virginia Judge* (1935), gave her roles that were strictly "sweet young things."

She made twelve films during her 1935-38 tenure, including two (*Gentle Julia* and *Annapolis Salute*) on loan-out. All her parts were pretty much the same, all cut from the same ingenue cloth. But she never complained. "It was not in my nature to rebel. I simply did the best I knew how with what I was given to do. Whether I was growing in the process, I'm not in the position to judge. I did feel at Paramount that everything they gave me was somewhat similar to all the others, with only a change of wardrobe, a change of title, or a change of leading man. But it was pretty much the same formula." Formula or not, Marsha projected a great charm in these films. They demanded little from her.

But films like *The Arizona Raiders* (1936), *Hollywood Boulevard* (1936), and *Murder Goes to College* (1937) weren't providing her with what she sought: "A role that had some color, some body to it, a challenge."

One prominent event during her Paramount days was her marriage to Jerry Hopper, then assistant head of the studio's music department. She left Paramount, she said, after a year of inactivity, in June of '38. The couple was wed in November of that year; the marriage would end in a 1945 divorce.

She freelanced briefly at the poverty row studios, but wound up at MGM for *The Hardys Ride High* (1939). It was a mere two-minute bit as a spendthrift wife, but it alerted MGM to her possibilities. They wanted her to test for a juicy part in their upcoming production *These Glamour Girls*, to star Lana Turner and Lew Ayres.

"That was the first real acting role I feel that I got," Marsha told this writer in 2002. "Paramount gave me nothing but romantic leads. Imagine starting at seventeen at the top like that—but the parts were all sweet young nothings. No reality or interest or character to them. After twelve of those, Paramount and I parted. Then it was Metro giving me *These Glamour Girls*, with me as this kind of neurotic college widow who is desperate to catch the right husband before it's too late. It was fun to do, and it started a whole chain of no-two-alike-roles. I then had the time of my life."

This stunning piece of acting led to further parts at MGM. "I vanished into my roles," Hunt proudly told historian Anthony Slide in 1999, "projecting as little of myself as possible from one role to another. They were vastly different, and so was I... That early title I was given at Metro as 'Hollywood's Youngest Character Actress' is the proudest thing I can record. I played four old ladies before I was thirty, a Brooklyn showgirl, society snob, schoolteacher, unmarried mother, army nurse, two nightclub singers, crime lab technician, spoiled heiress, symphony harpist, farm girl, and two suicides, among others."

MGM began using her so much, they finally put her under contract. She alternated between leads in their B movies (including the sweet *I'll Wait for You*, and the sleepers *Joe Smith, American* and *Kid Glove Killer*) to feature roles in the studio's big films (*Blossoms in the Dust*, *Cry Havoc*, *The Human Comedy*). MGM also, on occasion, gave her some well-deserved showcases for her considerable comedic abilities: *Pride and Prejudice* (1940) and *The Affairs of Martha* (1942). "I wasn't interested in stardom," Hunt pointed out later. "It wasn't the pinnacle I was after. I wanted to be a good actress. I just wanted to be stretched to the limit and to grow in the process, and so I was ecstatic at MGM."

Marsha Hunt was going nicely along with films like *None Shall Escape* (1944), *The Valley of Decision* (1945), *Smash-Up, the Story of a Woman* (1947) and the *noir* classic *Raw Deal* (1948), when her career took a downward turn.

It was during this time that Hollywood came under the attack of the House Un-American Activities Committee. Just being *suspected* of being a Communist was enough to get you blacklisted. When the "Hollywood Ten," a group of writers and directors, were jailed in October of 1947 for refusing to "name names" and explain their political beliefs, pleading the First Amendment, a group of actors headed to Washington, D.C. to protest the action. Marsha, along with her husband, since 1946, writer Robert Presnell, Jr., joined the celebrity group headed by Humphrey Bogart and Lauren Bacall to speak out on behalf of the Ten.

"That and similar positions resulted in my being blacklisted," Marsha said later, "and I was unable to find work in films, radio, or television. Somehow, the live theater remained free of this witch hunt. From 1948 to 1950 I was in New York City doing Broadway plays [including *Joy to the World* with Alfred Drake] and a lot of early television."

She was listed in the right-wing publication *Red Channels* in 1950, and she saw her film, radio and television career stop "dead in its tracks. After some years, it resumed somewhat, but never with the same momentum."

Her films were sporadic during the fifties, mostly playing mothers, in projects like *The Happy Time* (1952) and *Blue Denim* (1959). Both films showed her versatility; she gave a charming, light performance in the former, and a powerfully intense one in the latter. Marsha was almost cast as James Dean's mother in *Rebel without a Cause*, but had to bow out at the last minute because of a prior stage commitment.

Hunt stayed busy on television through the years, picking up speed in the sixties (as the Blacklist started to lift) with appearances on *The Defenders, Ben Casey, Marcus Welby, M.D.* (with former MGM co-star Robert Young), and *Police Story*, among others. Her last TV gig was on a 1988 episode of *Star Trek: The Next Generation. Johnny Got His Gun* (1971) was her last theatrically-released film.

Despite the detour forced upon her by The Blacklist, Marsha remained true to herself. When offers dried up in Hollywood, she went to New York. She did stage work, in New York and on tour, and kept doing it into the 1990s (*On Golden Pond*). Her talent couldn't be stalled by political roadblocks.

Today, Marsha is still active in raising money for charities and is a welcome guest at film conventions. She first published her book *The Way We Wore* in 1996, and has just republished it in 2003; it is a lavish tome devoted to the fashions she (and others) wore during the thirties and forties.

Like Marsha Hunt herself, it is elegant, classy and timeless.

Virginia Grey
by Laura Wagner

By the time she played on TV version of *The Bickersons* in the fifties, Virginia Grey had been a show business vet for over twenty years. She had made her first appearance before the cameras at the age of nine, playing "Little Eva" in *Uncle Tom's Cabin* (1927).

Virginia was born on March 22, 1917 in Edendale, California. "It was in Edendale that the first movie colony in the West was established, and for five prosperous years made moving-picture history," said actor Coy Watson, Jr., who also grew up there during this period of early moviemaking. It was in Edendale that Mack Sennett made his first comedies. In the center of all this was Virginia's father, Ray Grey. Virginia's early years were spent watching her father go from being a Keystone Kop to assistant (*Molly O*), then full-fledged director of shorts and features (*Among Those Present, Down on the Farm, Andy Takes a Flyer*). She remembered being babysat by Gloria Swanson.

When her father died suddenly in 1925, of pneumonia, Virginia's mother, to support her three daughters, went to work at Universal as a film cutter. It was on that lot that Virginia was spotted by producer Paul Kohner, and was screen tested for *Uncle Tom's Cabin*. From there, she played roles in *The Michigan Kid, Heart to Heart* and *Jazz Mad* (all 1928).

She struggled mostly in the thirties, getting small roles here and there. It wasn't until her dance bit in The *Great Ziegfeld* (1936) that things started to look up. Impressed by her beauty, she was signed by MGM at $50 a week..

Virginia's years at MGM were wholly unremarkable. They never gave her that "break-out" role that would propel her to stardom. She had considerable ability, and was able to make much out of what they gave her in such films as *Bad Guy* (1937), *The Hardy's Ride High* (striking as a con artist), *Another Thin Man*, *The Women* (all three 1939), *Hullabaloo* (1940), and *The Big Store* (1941). Her roles seemed to indicate that MGM didn't know what to do with her. *Whistling in the Dark* (1941), with Red Skelton and Ann Rutherford, was clear evidence that her forte was in comedy; her sparkling presence in that film was delightful, but she was too gorgeous for such silly shenanigans—or so the studio thought. They cast her more as "the other woman," the menace that the leading lady had to watch out for. She was at her bitchest in the later *Flame of Barbary Coast* (1945).

After she left MGM in '42, she remained extremely busy. Virginia freelanced for every studio, big and small, and never seemed to take a breather. Her later work included *Sweet Rosie O'Grady* (1943), *Swamp Fire* (1946), *Unconquered* (1947), *Who Killed Doc Robbin?*, *Unknown Island* (both 1948, and rare leads), *Mexican Hayride* (1948—a fun performance), *The Threat* (1949), *Bullfighter and the Lady* (1951), *The Fighting Lawman* (1953—in a super portrayal of a unscrupulous woman), *Target Earth* (1954), *The Rose Tattoo* (1955), *All that Heaven Allows* (1956), *Portrait in Black* (1960), and *Tammy Tell Me True* (1961). It is said that she has made at least 200 movies. Producer Ross Hunter considered her a "good luck charm," and cast her in nine of his films.

Television was also a steady, *very* steady, source of work for her, starting in 1948 and progressing unfailingly until 1969. She was seen on such diverse shows as *The Jack Benny Show*, *General Electric Theatre*, *Wagon Train*, *Jane Wyman Presents*, *The Millionaire*, *Peter Gunn*, *Bonanza*, *My Three Sons*, *I Spy* and *Love, American Style*.

She retired in the seventies after three more films appearances (*Airport*, the TV movie *The Lives of Jenny Dolan*, and the mini-series *Arthur Hailey's The Moneychangers*) and stage work (*Sugar and Spice* with John Ireland).

Grey, who never married, is known today for her long-running relationship with Clark Gable, who loved her down-to-earth quality, a quality that moviegoers equally found appealing onscreen. Virginia might not have been a star, but she was a beautiful, hardworking, more than capable actress.

Danny Thomas, founder of St. Jude Children's Research Hospital.

Danny Thomas

Danny "Brother Amos" Thomas was born Muzyad Yakhoob in Deerfield, Michigan on January 6, 1912. Most biographies of this great nightclub comic usually omit his part in The Bickersons since it (and *Drene Time* itself) was such a minor achievement in his illustrious radio and television career.

He started his career as a singer, vocalizing over a Detroit radio station in 1932. Six years later he hit nightclubs, doubling as an MC-comedian. Beginning as stand-up comic "Amos Jacobs," he excelled in dialect comedy (Yiddish, Lebanese, Italian and Irish) with an emphasis on storytelling with an "ironic" conclusion. After touring clubs in the Midwest, in the early 1940s he landed a three-year stint in Chicago's prestigious 5100 Club where the powerful William Morris Agency soon picked up his contract. Under the wing of his mentor "Uncle" Abe Lastfogel, Thomas began playing the best nightclubs in New York. After a successful USO tour with Marlene Dietrich, he worked on Fanny Brice's radio show. It was there that he met Philip Rapp who decided to make Thomas a part of his new *Drene Time* creation. By 1946 he was hot: he was voted "best newcomer in radio" in the national newspapers.

His film career wasn't prestigious. Danny had good chances with roles in *The Unfinished Dance* (1947), *Big City* (1948), *Call Me Mister* (1951), *I'll See You in My Dreams* (1951, playing songwriter Gus Kahn), and nabbing Al Jolson's role in the remake of *The Jazz Singer* (1953), but he failed to click on the big screen.

It would be television which would earn Danny his reputation, and long-lasting popularity. He co-starred with Jimmy Durante, Jack Carson and Ed Wynn on NBC's *Four Star Review* from 1950 to 1952. The next year saw his most significant contribution to the medium.

Make Room for Daddy was a semi-autobiographical sitcom suggested by Danny's wife Rose Marie Cassaniti. The series began in 1953 and won a number of awards, including Emmys in 1953 ("Best New Program") and 1954 ("Best Situation Comedy Series"), plus a '54 Emmy for himself as Best Actor in a Series. After the fourth season, "wife" Jean Hagen left the series, altering the format to Danny's being a widower with children looking for a new mate; she would be eventually replaced by Marjorie Lord. The hit stayed on television, changing its name to *The Danny Thomas Show* in 1957, until Thomas took it off the air in 1964 while it was still a top-rated show.

During the run he and movie gangster Sheldon Leonard teamed up to establish Thomas-Leonard Productions, responsible for such mega-hits as *The Andy Griffith Show* (a spin-off of a *Make Room for Daddy* episode) and *The Dick Van Dyke Show*. He later teamed up with Aaron Spelling to create and produce *The Mod Squad* and other shows. Attempts to revive his own show failed, with the quick cancellations of *The Danny Thomas Hour* (1967-68) and *Make Room for Granddaddy (1970-71)*, which reunited the original cast of *Make Room for Daddy*. He was inducted into the A.T.A.S. (Academy of Television Arts and Sciences) Hall of Fame, which was formed in 1984.

Throughout his television years he was also a concerned philanthropist, always interested in helping children. He received a profusion of humanitarian awards, including the Michelangelo Award from Boys Town of Italy, the Father Flanagan Boys Town Award, and, in 1984, the Congressional Medal of Honor. His major achievement was founding St. Jude Children's Research Hospital in 1962. He was even nominated for the Nobel Peace Prize in 1980-81. He died in Los Angeles (of a heart attack) on February 6, 1991. His daughter, actress Marlo Thomas (*That Girl* on television) continues her father's humanitarian pursuits.

Unused Material

Jokes Not Used (some were written for Don and Marsha on Edgar Bergen's show)

BLANCHE: He phones his wife 12 times a day. Why don't you do that?
JOHN: I don't know her number.

BLANCHE: I'm worried that I lost your love.
JOHN: Stop worrying about trifles.

BLANCHE: It's a chocolate-date-salad-tutti-fruiti-marshmellow-cherry-hot-butterscotch sundae. Do you want anything on it or will you eat it plain?

BLANCHE: Well, don't talk when I'm trying to interrupt.

JOHN: You always were a fault-finder.
BLANCHE: I found you, dear.

BLANCHE: Do I buy clothes like Gloria Gooseby? No. Did I buy three new hats last Easter? No. Did I borrow fifty dollars from a loan company to pay my bridge debts?
JOHN: No.
BLANCHE: Yes, I did.

BLANCHE: Did you rock the cat to sleep?

JOHN: I rocked the cat, I clubbed the canary and I drowned the goldfish.

BLANCHE: Dr. Hersey has given his young wife two days to live?
JOHN: Really?
BLANCHE: Yeah, he went out of town for a couple of days.

BLANCHE: There's nothing wrong with that cheese. It was imported from Switzerland.
JOHN: Tastes more like it was deported.

JOHN: I suppose you're still angry because I came home late last night with this black-eye.
BLANCHE: Maybe you've forgotten, but when you came home, you didn't have that black-eye.

DOC: I can't find any cause for your complaint. I think it's due to drinking.
JOHN: All right, I'll come back sometime when you're sober.

JOHN: Wish we had a fifth for bridge.
BLANCHE: Nobody has a fifth for bridge.
JOHN: All right—make it a pint then.

BLANCHE: How can I tell toadstools from mushrooms?
JOHN: Eat some before you go to bed. If you wake up the next morning, they're mushrooms.

BLANCHE: I wonder if I could make you melt in my arms.
JOHN: No, I'm not that soft and you're not that hot.

JOHN: Just because I was in the middle of the road on my hands and knees is no sign I was drunk.
BLANCHE: I know—but you were trying to roll up the white line.

BLANCHE: Dear, have you eaten any sandwiches?

JOHN: Yes. They were very nice. Why?
BLANCHE: Oh, nothing—only I suppose you'll have to clean your brown shoes with meat paste tomorrow.

JOHN: Did you win a prize with your cake?
BLANCHE: Not exactly, but I got horrible mention.

BLANCHE: You ought to make that Barney learn a trade so that he'll at least know what kind of work he's out of.

BLANCHE: Why don't you like the way Gloria dresses?
JOHN: I think she wears her skirt too high.
BLANCHE: Well, what of it? She has a perfect right.
JOHN: Yes, and her left isn't bad, either.

BLANCHE: I never had any hard luck till I married you. My whole family has always been so lucky. Look at my Uncle Willy.
JOHN: What's so lucky about him?
BLANCHE: Well, he was operated on for the removal of a pearl he accidentally swallowed while eating oysters, and when the pearl was examined it was found to be valuable enough to pay for both the operation and the funeral.

BLANCHE: I do everything to save money for you. Last winter I knitted you socks out of that old bathing suit of yours, and this summer I knitted myself a bathing suit out of your old socks.

JOHN: The first time I kissed a girl I thought I was supposed to marry her. That's how dumb I was.
BLANCHE: What's so dumb about that?
JOHN: I married her.

(After giving Cabbie exact fare)
BLANCHE: That's correct, isn't it?

CABBIE: It's correct, lady—but it ain't right.

JOHN: I wish I was dead!
BLANCHE: I wish I was, too.
JOHN: Then I don't wish I was.

(They have agreed not to talk to each other...but she starts talking and gets no reply)
BLANCHE: John!
JOHN: Mmm.
BLANCHE: You might at least have the courtesy to say "shut up."

BLANCHE: Remember how I've been bothering you about moving to a more expensive apartment?
JOHN: Well, we don't have to move. The landlord just raised the rent.

(On phone)
JOHN: Blanche, have you seen the notice of my death in the paper?
BLANCHE: Yes, dear...Where are you calling from?

BLANCHE: I think something's wrong with Mel Shaw. Sometimes Louise talks to him for hours and then discovers he literally hasn't heard a word she said. What do you suppose he's got?
JOHN: I don't know, but whatever it is, I'd like to borrow it.

BLANCHE: John, if I have my wisdom tooth extracted will it make me stupid?
JOHN: Blanche, the idea that wisdom teeth have anything to do with wisdom is ridiculous. If you were to have every tooth in your head extracted it couldn't make you any more stupid than you are right now.

JOHN: She dresses modestly and sensibly.
BLANCHE: Yes, that woman will do anything to attract attention.

MAN: My wife talks to herself a lot.
JOHN: So does mine, only she thinks I'm listening.

BLANCHE: Why don't you quit your drinking?
JOHN: I only drink to relieve my suffering.
BLANCHE: What are you suffering from?
JOHN: Thirst.

JOHN: The cost of living has gone up three dollars a bottle.

BLANCHE: Apartments aren't really so hard to find.
JOHN: No.
BLANCHE: No. I bet if I used my head I could find a vacancy.

JOHN: How do you know Lorraine loves her husband so much?
BLANCHE: Well, when she's away she writes letters to him whether she needs money or not.

BLANCHE: John, in your whole life did you ever try to get anything for me?
JOHN: Several times—but nobody would make me an offer.

BLANCHE: An old school friend asked to be remembered to you—a man called Robinson.
JOHN: Don't remember him.
BLANCHE: Short man with whiskers
JOHN: I never went to school with a short man with whiskers.

BLANCHE: I was so embarrassed when Donna opened all her lovely wedding presents. I wish we'd have given her something nicer.

JOHN: What we gave her was plenty nice. What's wrong with a silver-plated garbage can?
BLANCHE: Nothing – only you should have emptied it before you gave it to them.
JOHN: I just stuffed it with paper to keep it from scratching. None of the other gifts were so expensive—they got some monogrammed dental floss from the Auerbacks, a Hickock belt from the Hickocks—
BLANCHE: What did the Gooseby's give them?
JOHN: A goose. A 3 ½ pounder that Leo shot in Westlake Park.

BLANCHE: Did you remember to empty the water under the icebox?
JOHN: Yes, I emptied it and put in fresh water.

BLANCHE: Is there no hope, Doctor?
DOC: I don't know. What were you hoping for?

BLANCHE: I hope this diamond ring isn't a cheap imitation.
JOHN: What do you mean cheap? It's the most expensive imitation I could find.

BLANCHE: Is your bed lumpy?
JOHN: No.
BLANCHE: Is there a draft on you?
JOHN: No.
BLANCHE: Is your mattress comfortable?
JOHN: Yes.
BLANCHE: Well, will you change places with me?

BLANCHE: John, am I so hard to please?
JOHN: I don't know—I've never tried.

BLANCHE: Will you love me when I'm old and ugly?
JOHN: Of course I do.

BLANCHE: You married me for my money.
JOHN: Well, I earned it.

(In hotel)
BLANCHE: How much are your rooms?
MAN: From six dollars up to twelve.
BLANCHE: How much for all night?

JOHN: Blanche, drinking makes you beautiful.
BLANCHE: But I don't drink.
JOHN: No, but I do.

JOHN: Oh, don't worry about me when I go, Blanche. I'll write often.
BLANCHE: Do, darling, do—even if it's only a check.

BLANCHE: Look at this headline. "One Wife Too Many…" I guess it's about a bigamist.
JOHN: Not necessarily, dear.

BLANCHE: Could you give me a little shopping money, John?
JOHN: Certainly, dear. About how little?

BLANCHE: John, I want to see that letter.
JOHN: What letter, dear?
BLANCHE: That one you just opened. I know by the handwriting it's from a woman, and you turned pale when you read it. Hand it over.
JOHN: Here it is, dear. It's from your dressmaker.

BLANCHE: Why didn't you water the lawn yesterday?
JOHN: It was raining.
BLANCHE: That's no excuse, you've got a raincoat.

BLANCHE: I started out on the theory that the world had an opening for you.

JOHN: Well, I'm in a hole now.

BLANCHE: Married men like to drink. It makes them see double and feel single.

JOHN: Marriage is wonderful in the long run. After a year or two a man gets used to it and it's just as good as if he'd never been married at all.

BLANCHE: Oh, John, the landlord has raised the rent.
JOHN: Has he? I can't.

DOC: You are certainly kind to send your wife away for a rest.
JOHN: Yes, God knows I need it.

MAN: Does your husband carry life insurance?
BLANCHE: No, he just carries fire insurance. He knows where he's going.

BLANCHE: What are you looking for?
JOHN: Nothing.
BLANCHE: You'll find it in the bottle where the bourbon used to be.

BLANCHE: Anybody would think that I was nothing but a cook in this household!
JOHN: Not after eating a meal here.

BLANCHE: I saw you drinking at the wedding.
JOHN: Oh, that was only Punch.
BLANCHE: Punch, my eye!
JOHN: Don't tempt me.

BLANCHE: How many times did you propose to me before I accepted?

JOHN: Once too often.

JOHN: I'm afraid we'll have to manage differently, Blanche. I'm not making expenses.
BLANCHE: Don't worry about that. You just go on with your work and I'll make plenty of expenses.

JOHN: Did you set the mousetrap?
BLANCHE: Yes.
JOHN: Where is it?
BLANCHE: It's right where you can put your finger on it.

JOHN: I can speak Spanish, German, French, Italian, but there's one tongue I can't master.
BLANCHE: What's that?
JOHN: Yours.

BLANCHE: John, did anyone ever tell you how wonderful you are?
JOHN: Don't believe they ever did.
BLANCHE: Then where'd you get the idea?

MAN: This letter says that John is being divorced from his wife.
WOMAN: What happened? Did he walk out on her?
MAN: No, he walked in on her.

JOHN: How did Clara come to marry Barney?
BLANCHE: Oh, they just started out to be good friends and then changed their minds.

BLANCHE: You can't take the goldfish without the bowl. They need water.
JOHN: I'll spit on them all the way up there.

BLANCHE: The cat'll be lonesome in that bag.
JOHN: No, he won't—I put the canary in there with him.

BLANCHE: I found a five-dollar bill today, dear.
JOHN: All right, give it to me. I'll pay it.

BLANCHE: I think you've been a faithful husband, John. Not once since you married me have you done a wrong thing. Have you, darling?
JOHN: No, that was the last.

BLANCHE: Oh, you needn't think you're so wonderful. The night you proposed to me you looked absolutely silly.
JOHN: I was.

BLANCHE: Some of the girls were discussing how they met their husbands, and I couldn't remember. Where did you meet me, John?
JOHN: I didn't meet you—you overtook me.

BLANCHE: John, it's almost a year since our last anniversary and that glorious day we spent on the sands. I wonder how we'll spend this one?
JOHN: On the rocks.

JOHN: Is he married?
BLANCHE: No, but he's engaged—that's as good as being married.
JOHN: As good? It's a darned sight better.

BLANCHE: After seven years of married life, John, I've reached the conclusion that you don't love me—
JOHN: Now, Blanche –
BLANCHE: It's no use protesting. You should have married some ordinary, stupid girl.
JOHN: Well, darling, I did my best.

BLANCHE: Would you go into the war if there was another one?
JOHN: Yes, there's nothing I would enjoy so much as a little peace and quiet.

BLANCHE: And I hope someday to be able to dance on your grave.
JOHN: That's fine. I'll be buried at sea.

BLANCHE: It hurts every time I hit it with a spoon.
JOHN: Don't hit it.
BLANCHE: Then how can I tell it hurts?

JOHN: Women will never live to be a hundred.
BLANCHE: Why not?
JOHN: They stop too long at thirty.

BLANCHE: How do you want to announce dinner? Should we say, "Dinner is ready?" or "Dinner is served?"
JOHN: If it's anything like yesterday—just say dinner is burnt.

JOHN: I'm the only man in town who can put his socks on from both ends.

JOHN: I kissed that bride, didn't I?
BLANCHE: Yeah—but it was two years after the ceremony.

BLANCHE: Get me a hot water bag.
JOHN: You don't need it, don't be a sissy.
BLANCHE: Get it for me.
(He hands her hot water bag from his own bed)

BLANCHE: Where are you going?
JOHN: I'm gonna sleep in the bathtub.
BLANCHE: But there's water in it.
JOHN: What about it?
BLANCHE: Last time you fell asleep in the bathtub, you snored and the neighbors accused me of running an outboard motor.

JOHN: I'm so hungry I could eat the dicky off a penguin.

BLANCHE: These vitamin pills will increase your vitality.
JOHN: I don't want to increase it, I just want to hold onto what I've got.

BLANCHE: If it isn't too much trouble, tell me, am I the only one you ever kissed?
JOHN: Without too much trouble, yes.

BLANCHE: When I married you I didn't know you were such a coward. I thought you were a brave man.
JOHN: So did everybody else.

JOHN: We can't take a vacation. My account at the bank is overdrawn.
BLANCHE: Well, why don't you keep your account in a bank that has plenty of money?

BLANCHE: John, don't you think you should wear something to show people you're married?
JOHN: I do.
BLANCHE: What?
JOHN: A worried look.

BLANCHE: When you were courting me, you said you hated marriage. But then you saw your mistake and married me.
JOHN: You got that in reverse, Blanche.

BLANCHE: Before we were married you always gave me the most beautiful presents. Why don't you anymore?
JOHN: Ever hear of a fisherman giving bait to a fish after he caught it?

JOHN: You lied to me before we were married.
BLANCHE: What do you mean?
JOHN: When I asked you to marry me you said you were agreeable.

BLANCHE: I always know when you win at poker. You sleep with your pants on.

BLANCHE: Leo Gooseby always keeps his word.
JOHN: He has to—nobody else would take it.

BLANCHE: Remember, John, it takes two to make a marriage.
JOHN: In our case it was you and your mother.

JOHN: They say whiskey shortens a man's life, but he sees twice as much in the same length of time.

BLANCHE: Some men marry for love, and some men marry for money. John, why did you marry me?
JOHN: So you've begun to wonder, too.

JOHN: If I ever marry again I'll marry a woman that's easy to please.
BLANCHE: That's the only kind you'll be able to get.

BLANCHE: I was a fool to ever marry you.
JOHN: Now, now, dear, I won't let you take the blame for that. I was a fool for ever asking you.

JOHN: They may cut my salary in half. Darling, do you think you can manage on my salary of twenty dollars a week?
BLANCHE: I'll try—but what will *you* do?

BLANCHE: I need a new checkbook, John.
JOHN: What happened to your old one?
BLANCHE: I lost it. But I took the precaution of signing all the checks, so it won't be any use to anyone else.

JOHN: The doctor says I've been working too hard lately. He says I need a little sun and air.
BLANCHE: But honey, didn't you tell him we can't afford one yet?

JOHN: She's a perfect photograph of her father and a pretty good phonograph of her mother.

BLANCHE: Get my little fur choker.
JOHN: Where is it? Is this your choker? I've been letting it out every night for three weeks. I thought it was the cat.

BLANCHE: What did you do with the cake?
JOHN: I fed it to the cat.
BLANCHE: John Bickerson!
JOHN: That's all right, I'll get you another cat.

BLANCHE: Get up and let the cat in.
JOHN: Why don't you get him a key?

BLANCHE: When I can't afford something, I pay cash for it.

BLANCHE: If you act that way in my dreams, what do you do in yours?

BLANCHE: Listen, I'm sick of you saying *my* car, *my* house, *my* etc.—It's getting on my nerves and you've got to learn to say "our." What are you looking for?
JOHN: Our *pants*.

BLANCHE: Why are you two hours late?
JOHN: I was run over.
BLANCHE: It doesn't take two hours to be run over.

BLANCHE: You never think at all—that's the trouble with you. St. Valentine's Day came and went and what did I get from you?
JOHN: I sent you a Valentine and you know it!
BLANCHE: That horrible lace thing! It was awful!
JOHN: It was beautiful! I sat up half the night making it out of my old silk shorts! You got the only Valentine in town that buttons up the back.

BLANCHE: If you'd only try, you could get rid of that snoring. Why don't you take something for it?
JOHN: Make me an offer.

JOHN: Darling, I have to go to New York on business. It'll only be for two or three days and I hope you won't miss me while I'm gone.
BLANCHE: I won't, because I'm going with you.
JOHN: I wish you could. It won't be convenient. What do you want to go for anyway?
BLANCHE: I need new clothes.
JOHN: But you can get all the clothes you want right here on Main Street.
BLANCHE: Thank you. That's all I wanted.

BLANCHE: I mended that hole in your pocket last night after you'd gone to bed. Wasn't I thoughtful?
JOHN: Yes, but how did you discover there was a hole in my pocket?

(Doorbell rings)
LANG: John!
DON: Hmmm?
LANG: Somebody just rang the doorbell.
DON: Huh? Who rang the doorbell, Blanche?
LANG: I don't know.
(Doorbell rings)
LANG: He's ringing it again. It might be a burgler. What'll I do, John?
DON: Have a key made for him. Goodnight, Blanche.
LANG: Please, John—get up and see who it is. I'm frightened.
DON: Oh, don't be so scared. I'll see who it is.
LANG: You better take something to protect yourself with.
DON: Good idea. Where's my bourbon? Oh, here it is…(Clink of glass)
LANG: John, why are you taking a drink now of all times?

DON: You don't want me to hit him with a full bottle, do you?
LANG: Go on. Open the door.
DON: I'm going, I'm going. Where's that doorknob? (Sound of door opening) There's nobody here, Blanche.
LANG: You're looking in the closet.

BLANCHE: John, the other day the bank sent me a note saying I had overdrawn our account and they wanted fourteen dollars to balance it. I sent it to them right away—but they're still bothering me.
JOHN: You sent the fourteen dollars?
BLANCHE: The same day.
JOHN: That's strange. How did you send it?
BLANCHE: I sent them a check, of course.

BLANCHE: Where would you be if it wasn't for me?
JOHN: I don't know, but I wish I was there.

Situations not used:

DRIVING – She's hungry. Doesn't like any of the places he stops at.

She bought a new bathing suit.

Turtle-neck sweater soup.

Blanche has lost her wedding ring. Doesn't believe she's married without it. Has taken ads in all local papers, including a few out of town. Reviews places she's visited where she might have lost it—mostly department stores. On the way reveals she has spent a good deal of money in each store. He finally finds wedding ring in his pocket.

Blanche has taken option on ancient mansion atop Lookout Mountain. House is furnished, and is for sale very cheaply because of legend that place is haunted. Bickersons spend night there.

Opening:
The lawyer is concluding the reading of the will.
LAWYER: Goodnight.
BLANCHE: (Dismayed) What about me? You left my name out.
Lawyer assures her that she inherits nothing. He leaves. Blanche worries about John—how will he take it? He's waiting in his room anxiously.
FADE. JOHN SNORES.
Blanche enters. Wakes him.
BLANCHE: I've been cut off.
JOHN: Put another nickel in.

Vitamin B injection—bourbon.
Sleep on wedding cake.
John has to return tuxedo at 5 A.M., left his only suit as deposit.
Chickenschmidt the Butcher

Open with snore.

Foot tied to bedpost.

Noise of freezer—business of freezer stopping each time John approaches it.
Blanche's brother has been evicted—freezer belongs to him.
Strange foods in freezer. She puts his bourbon in it. "My God—a bourbon Popsicle."
Kicks freezer—glass crash—"I'm sorry. I want this mudhen for breakfast."
Phone rings—can't locate it—finally finds it in freezer. Speaks to boss—at finish can't pull phone from his ear.

Bickerson Ideas:

1. She comes home to find John sleeping. He was supposed to meet her at her sister's wedding right after work, but he fell asleep while putting on his tuxedo. He is sleeping in it.
2. She has been to a psychiatrist to find out why they fight so much. Twenty dollars a half-hour. Says they should sleep in different rooms.
3. Blanche has decided that John doesn't make enough money. So she is going to get a job. She has all the newspapers on the bed and is going through the want ads. Calls one boss in the middle of the night.

Index

Allen, Steve, 2, 125
Ameche, Don, i, 1-3, 24-25, 28-44, 55, 57, 66-67, 69, 77, 110, 128-129, 133, 144, 149, 163, 177, 185, 191, 193, 199-201, 206-207, 210, 225
Bare, Richard L., 116
Bergen, Edgar (*The Charlie McCarthy Show*), 28, 57-58, 67, 225
Blake, Whitney, 150, 155, 157, 161, 163
Brice, Fanny, 24, 195, 223
Bryant, Josh, 150, 155, 157, 159-161, 166
Carson, Jack, 2, 223
cartoon series, 173-176
Cavalcade of Stars, 115, 119-120, 206, 211
Columbia Records, 131, 133, 141, 201
Como, Perry, 2, 129, 131, 133, 207
Conte, John, 70-85
Crosby, John, 30, 56
Dalton, Abby, 161-163, 166
Dragon, Carmen, 28-29, 32-38, 42-43, 55
Drene Time, 24-25, 28-32, 58, 121, 201, 206, 223
Forest, George, 70, 72
Forman, Joey, 161-162, 166
Gardiner, Reginald, 70, 77-85
Gleason, Jackie, 65, 114-125, 211
Goodman, Benny, 69, 211
Grey, Virginia, 113-114, 117, 219-220
Hollywood Palace, 2, 131, 146, 207
Honeymooners, The, 118-123, 131
Hope, Bob, i, 8, 24-25, 30, 70, 204-207, 210
Hunt, Marsha, 3, 57-58, 206, 214-217, 225
Kaye, Danny, 24, 56, 122, 149, 195
Kean, Betty, 56, 66, 125, 129, 211
Langford, Frances, ix-x, 1-3, 24-25, 29-38, 43-44, 55-57, 67, 69-77, 82-83, 91, 111-112, 114, 128-131, 133, 135, 141-146, 149, 165, 167-168, 177, 185, 191, 202-207, 210
Match Please, Darling, 147-166
Miller, Marvin, 28-29, 32-34, 41-44, 55
Moore, Del, 150, 159-161, 164
Morgan, Frank, 31-33, 36-43, 55, 206

Old Gold Show, The, 32-56, 67, 72, 119, 133
Parker, Lew, 2, 17, 56, 65-67, 69-79, 86, 91, 110-117, 120-121, 125-126, 129, 144, 163, 201, 209-212
"Philip Morris," 110-113
"Please Go 'Way and Let Me Sleep," 25-28
Rapp, Joel, 3, 55, 57, 147-166, 193, 196
Rapp, John, 25, 70
Rapp, Mary, 24
Rapp, Paul, 2, 114, 188-193, 211
Rapp, Philip, i, 2, 21, 24-25, 28, 30-32, 55-57, 65, 67, 69-71, 75-77, 110-112, 114-118, 121-126, 128-129, 131, 133, 135, 142, 144, 146-147, 149-154, 162, 164, 168, 173-177, 186-196, 223
Saturday Night Revue, 117-118

Shayne, Gloria, 135-136
Shaw, Mel, 21, 25, 154, 166, 228
Spilton, Alan, 135-136
Spring in Brazil, 70, 195
Star Time, 69-110
Stewart, Martha, 65-66, 121
Sullivan, Ed, 2, 119, 121, 128, 211
Thomas, Danny, 1, 25, 28-30, 32, 212, 222-224
Tuttle, Lurene, 57, 111
Two Sleepy People, 56, 123
Wright, Robert, 70, 72
"You Say It (But You Won't Do It)," 135-142

Available now from

www.bearmanormedia.com

Buy the original recordings at
www.bickersons.com

www.ingramcontent.com/pod-product-compliance
Lightning Source LLC
Chambersburg PA
CBHW062014220426
43662CB00010B/1320